THE PERSONAL UNIVERSE

Essays in Honor of John Macmurray

> All meaningful knowledge is for the sake of action and all meaningful action for the sake of friendship.
>
> (John Macmurray, *Self As Agent*)

THE PERSONAL UNIVERSE

Essays in Honor of John Macmurray

Edited by

Thomas E. Wren

HUMANITIES PRESS   Atlantic Highlands, N.J.

1975

Library of Congress Cataloging in Publication Data
Main entry under title:

John Macmurray's search for reality.

"Reprinted from the spring 1975 issue of Listening."
Includes bibliographical references.
1. Macmurray, John, 1891-   —Addresses, essays,
lectures. 2. Philosophy, Modern—Addresses, essays,
lectures. I. Wren, Thomas E. II. Listening.
B1647.M134J6   192   75-20225
ISBN 0-391-00398-4

Reprinted from *Listening*, Journal
of Religion and Culture, Spring 1975.
Published in book form by Humanities Press, Inc.
with permission of the editors of *Listening*

Printed in the United States of America

CONTENTS

John Macmurray's Search for Reality: Introduction/

One of the truly universal figures of human existence is that of the Search. Picaresque accounts of what it means to be human recur continually in ancient and modern, Eastern and Western literatures, with varying degrees of specificity as to the object of the search: Penelope, lands of milk and honey, the Holy Grail, *il paradiso, die Heimat,* An Author, even the thrill of the chase itself. But the problem of what Ernst Bloch has called man's transcendental hunger is not that it is a lack, but that it is indeterminate. It might seem that when applied to human existence in general the metaphor of searching is vacuous, that by symbolizing everything it symbolizes nothing. But it is not vacuous, since the search in question is a search for reality, and it is a courageous undertaking precisely because there is a real risk of failure. The reflective man knows, and is sobered by his knowledge, that his search can very well end in the bitterest sort of unreality, with no chance of another try.

The philosopher who is honored in these pages, John Macmurray, has carried out a robust search for reality that has made full use of his scientific, aesthetic, and religious experiences and the categories derived from reflection on these experiences. His philosophical conception of reality is "religious" in his own sense of that word, which is roughly equivalent to interpersonal; the other main forms of knowledge—science and art—are subordinate albeit methodologically self-contained dimensions of interpersonal communion. Hence A.R.C. Duncan points out below that the title of Macmurray's partly autobiographical essay *Search for Reality in Religion* "is virtually descriptive of his entire life."

Exactly how this is so is shown by Duncan, whose valuable account of the intellectual background of Macmurray's Gifford Lectures is based on conversations with him as well as on his earlier works, and by Albert Nephew, who takes up the themes of the Gifford Lectures directly. As Duncan says, Macmurray's dominating philosophical concern has been to show how the divine element in the universe is personal. But Macmurray's way of doing this was to effect a "new Copernican Revolution," not unlike that wrought by Marx (whom Macmurray took quite seriously), in which philosophy is done from the standpoint of the socially implanted agent rather than that of the asocial, ahistorical, unembodied thinker. How this shift of standpoint transforms our notion of the divine is the point of Macmurray's Gifford Lectures, as Nephew concisely shows.

These lectures, separately published as *The Self as Agent* and *Persons in Relation* (their joint title, *The Form of the Personal*, is seldom used), are Macmurray's best-known works. This is as it should be, for in the tradition of the famous Gifford Lectureship he has produced a sustained intellectual symphony which, although necessarily "unfinished," is nevertheless an authoritative statement of what is now often called personalism. The list of Gifford lecturers is long and illustrious, including for instance John Dewey, Gabriel Marcel, and two other contributors to these pages besides Macmurray, namely W. H. F. Barnes and H. D. Lewis. Varied though their philosophical and religious convictions are, each lecturer has articulated his own search for reality—in religion or outside of it, as the case may be—in the process of fulfilling the conditions of the Gifford Lectureship.

In his own contribution to our collection John Macmurray has reaffirmed his abiding respect for that search for reality which is called science. He returns to science—not to its conclusions, but to its exercise—in order to illuminate the whole field of the personal. The personal is intrinsically objective, because in its reflecting and its acting the Self is necessarily correlative to an Other. Although the objectivity of science is empirical, its very empirical character opposes any a priori conflation of the physical, biological, and personal sciences into one superscience. Rather, each has its own subject matter and so its own methodology; in the case of the personal sciences this subject matter includes the fact of personal self-determination, with all the methodological problems that this unruly fact presents.

More important than his taxonomy of science, however, is Macmurray's double thesis: that the sciences always refer us beyond themselves, and that their glory is not that they are certain but rather that they necessarily regard as tentative whatever they have accomplished. Other forms of knowledge, equally subject to revision although less empirical than science, are not undermined by the scientific enterprise once its objectivity is understood, but are secured by Macmurray's distinction between objectivity and certainty. In art, philosophy, and even religion, the center of interest is displaced—just as it is in science—from the self to the object. That is, science is a paradigm of self-transcendence.

A somewhat different vein of the philosophy of science is worked by Errol Harris, who like Macmurray understands the universe as knowable order rather than as unknowable chaos. He too is inclined to push the search for reality all the way to religion (like Macmurray he delivered the Terry Lectures on religion at Yale); in his essay here he examines the attempts of those who, in the name of science, discard the metaphysical principle of teleology or orderedness, and concludes that "as teleology seems to be the only viable option for the metaphysician, theism of some sort is unavoidable." This and his other conclusions as well as his point of departure are akin to those of Macmurray's *Interpreting the Universe* especially (cited at the end of Harris's essay), although his intervening arguments are considerably different. To those who dismiss teleology as "mere metaphysics," Harris replies that this dismissal is equally metaphysical, that it would have to base itself on some general character of things as well as on some general rules of evidence. In other words, metaphysics is inescapable. To those who admit the viability of metaphysics but not that of teleology, Harris has several ripostes, the most fatal of which is probably his argument against thinking of the universe as purely random movement: movement implies moving particles or elements, which is to say (since modern physics knows nothing of elementary particles prior to energy systems in which the particles exist and move) an ordered system. And *voilà!*—orderedness and teleology once again.

The essays by Barnes and Lewis are contributed to this collection with the intention of honoring Macmurray, but they are not directly about him or his philosophy. Barnes's essay on Hobbes, whose significance in its own right is obvious to any student of the history of philosophy, is a fitting intellectual presentment to Macmurray principally because it confirms the latter's conviction that a natural, or as Barnes puts it, a *rational* theology is possible. Hobbes's own rational theology was, in Barnes's interpretation, that both the existence and the order of the world require a first Cause; Macmurray's is that a universe which was not united by a conception of God as person rather than as cause would be rationally as well as emotionally intolerable. But the two positions are not altogether opposed, for whatever their differences in standpoint might be, both Hobbes and Macmurray are inhabitants of the same universe. Hence Barnes appropriately glosses his final remark with the report that Hobbes regarded "cheerful, charitable and upright behaviour towards men" as "better signs of religion than the zealous maintaining of controverted doctrines"—a judgment that coincides exactly with Macmurray's conception of religious action and reflection.

So also does the general thesis of Lewis's essay, that a sound appreciation of what it means to be a person is a necessary condition for understanding practical interpersonal issues. Our regard for persons, which is to say for the personal Other, is rooted in our pre-philosophical knowledge that the intimacy between a person and his experience is as undeniable as it is ineffable or, as Lewis has it, "elusive." Although he opposes the quietistic tendencies of Western religions, he is particularly wary of the collectivistic tendencies of the great monistic religions of the East, on the grounds that there is no absorption of the individual person in the being of another, whether man or God. Religion, in short, is no refuge from social responsibility.

For Macmurray the search for reality includes not only the scientific quest (as his and Harris's essays show) and that of religion (as Duncan's and Nephew's essays show explicitly, Barnes's and Lewis's implicitly), but also what for lack of a more precise term we may call the ethical quest. This is shown in the essays by Axel Stern and Basil O'Leary, who use Macmurray's notions of value and justice respectively as points of departure for their own ethical searches. At this point a problem which has been smoldering flares up: what is the reference of the word "religion" for Macmurray? For Stern, who admits to having been strongly influenced by the logical positivism of the Vienna Circle, and for O'Leary, who regards natural law as just that, *natural* and not supernatural, Macmurray's remarks about religious experience and reflection would often be better expressed in terms of *ethical* categories. This revision, which seems to be a substantive one and not just a matter of semantics, seems to me to be quite proper although I shall not defend it here. But it is surely correct to say that whatever differences there are in Macmurray's thought between religion and ethics, the two are experienced and conceived of symbiotically by the moral/religious agent.

Stern's rather fine-grained argument for the rationality of human dignity involves a conception of intrinsic value which he clarifies at the outset of his essay, but which corresponds to a pre-philosophical notion we all have of things being good in themselves. The phenomenon of human dignity, he goes on to argue, arises as a result of our inevitable interdependence on each other: each of us not only attaches intrinsic values to things —that is, has purposes—but also recognizes that the rest of us do the same. Since valuing things includes valuing the autonomy of my valuation, and since there is no difference between this autonomy in my case and in yours, it follows that I must not only recognize your freedom but also respect it. Fully understood, my dignity consists in not only the qualities of autonomy and purposefulness, but also that of having moral respect for these qualities in others. Dignity, as Stern uses the term, is not an inert thing which one possesses but rather an activity which one does. It is a reflexive valuation of the capacity—in others as well as in oneself—to attribute intrinsic values to things. Human dignity presupposes as well as promotes human community.

But the universe is so constituted that community always takes place under conditions of scarcity, giving rise to the practical problems of society. These are primarily economic problems of production and consumption. But they are also problems of justice, since not all distributions are morally acceptable. O'Leary, himself an economist as well as a philosopher, argues that what Macmurray has called "a sense of justice" regarding the adequacy of a society (an essentially economic network) as a means toward community (a personal network) must be structured or "informed" by reason. The present global famine is so massive as to anesthetize our sense of justice unless that sense of justice has a rational base capable of generating rules of rightness appropriate to the ever new historical realities. This rational base, which is not itself a normative system but which is a necessary condition for a truly moral one, is, O'Leary concludes, an improved form of natural law. Such a natural law theory, cut free of Stoic and rationalistic premises, is an elaboration in the ethical realm of Macmurray's striking sentence: "All meaningful knowledge is for the sake of action, and all meaningful action for the sake of friendship."

Special acknowledgment and thanks are due to Loyola University of Chicago and its Philosophy Department for having provided assistance in preparing this Festschrift for publication, as well as to Mrs. Dona O'Brien and to Mr. Mark Frayne, who also helped correct the proofs.

THOMAS E. WREN

Science and Objectivity/

JOHN MACMURRAY

One of the changes in philosophical usage since I began to teach philosophy at the end of the first world war, is the rise to special prominence of the concept of objectivity. Where the contrast of objectivity and subjectivity now holds the field, we should have been discussing, fifty years ago, the contrast of truth and falsity. Indeed, I have sometimes thought, in reading contemporary philosophy, that the term "objective" was being used as a synonym for "true." This it can, of course, never be; it is at most an alternative, with an important modality of meaning.

In my efforts to bring my own usage up to date, this change became associated in my mind with another, which is undoubtedly of major importance. I refer to the change that has taken place in the philosophical valuation of science. One of my last memories of my time as an Oxford don is a confrontation of philosophers and scientists on the subject, to which I was invited. The traditional orthodoxy among philosophers was the view that science could hardly be called, in the strict sense, knowledge; only, at most, a systematic presentation of more or less well supported beliefs. The Idealists, still in the ascendant, though under heavy challenge, were prepared to admit that science was a first approximation to knowledge, but no more. For its radically hypothetical character refuted any claim to be knowledge in the full sense, since the concept of knowledge implied certainty. This was the view maintained at the meeting by the senior philosophers, and it was summed up by one of them at the end, as the result of many years of reflection upon the issue, in which the contentions of the scientists in the opposite sense had been carefully considered. To this the most vocal of the scientists replied, if I remember correctly, "Well! thank you for your exposition. I can only hope that you will go on thinking the matter over for some more years, and that you will come to a more sensible conclusion."

I myself left the gathering in a state of revolt, having always been a staunch supporter of science. It seemed to me that to maintain that science was not knowledge in the fullest sense was simply stupid, and that if the ruling theory of knowledge led to such ridiculous conclusions the sooner it was superseded the better. I found later that a number of the younger philosophers shared my reaction. There is no need for me to enlarge on the transformation that has actually taken place in the past half century. I should be surprised to find that any of us now doubted the claim of science to be in the fullest sense knowledge. But changes in fashion, whether in ladies' draperies or in philosopher's theories, often have a tendency to swing to the opposite extreme; and there are among us those who would go to the length of asserting, or implying, that *only* science is knowledge in the full sense, which to my thinking is just as stupid as its contrary which we have left behind.

I have come to think that it is the change in our valuation of science that underlies our new stress on objectivity. For even if we are convinced that science is knowledge in the fullest sense, it remains the case that it is thoroughly hypothetical. Science grows by moving from hypothesis to more adequate hypothesis, and the price we have to pay for this continual advance is to abandon the hope of certainty. For what we call, with subjective hopefulness, "verification," though it can prove a hypothesis false, can never prove it true. At most we can satisfy ourselves that none of the evidence available enables us, at the moment, to go beyond it. This is the glory of science, that it can never accept the point it has reached as the final certainty. Its business is to strive to surpass it.

I should like to pause here for a moment to stress the philosophical consequence of this change. We assert that science is proper knowledge, and what guarantees this is its objectivity.

Truth, and the avoidance of error, is the goal at which it aims, and the goal is set at an infinite distance; or perhaps better, truth defines a direction of advance, to which no end can be set. The maintaining of objectivity is also the condition of this advance. These are important conclusions. But more important still is the ground upon which the possibility of these assertions rests. *Knowledge does not imply certainty.* And if we accept this in the case of science, we must not demand certainty elsewhere as a condition of knowledge.

I propose now to try to go further towards an understanding of objectivity by a consideration of science in its larger branches. We might begin by reminding ourselves that there is no science in general, but only a continually increasing number of sciences. However, they fall naturally into three groups — the sciences of the inorganic, or physical sciences; the sciences of the organic, or biological sciences; and the sciences of the human, or personal sciences. These three groups were, as we know, established successively; but this is by no means a merely historical order. It is rather a difference in the subject matter, which makes the founding of the biological sciences more difficult than that of the physical ones, and the founding of the human sciences more so than that of the biological. In all three cases there were strong subjective resistances to be overcome, the resistance to biology being stronger than the resistance to physics, and the resistance to psychology stronger still. But the objective difficulties were more fundamental. They arise from the differences in subject matter, which present problems in method and organisation to be overcome. It is these differences of subject matter which I want to explore now, especially in their bearing upon objectivity. It might be helpful to consider these differences from the point of view of the levels of abstraction at which the different groups of sciences work. The physical sciences are concerned to investigate and understand a world in which there is no life of any kind. Biology introduces life, but no rationality. Only at the human level do we face a completely concrete world. For a human being is a physical object, he is a living creature, and he is a rational being. If anyone objects to my old-fashioned reference to rationality, I could say more clumsily, that man is a being capable of producing science.

The first thing to remark about the physical sciences is that their range of operation covers all observable entities, including organisms and persons, insofar as they are physical. I mean that the science of organic chemistry is a branch of chemistry, not of biology; and similarly human biology is a branch of biology, carrying with it the organic chemistry which is a branch of physical science. Perhaps it is this that provides the subjective origin of the reductionist illusion, which hopes in the long run — whenever that may be — to include all the sciences in the physical group. It would, perhaps, have been better if the term "science" had been reserved for the physical sciences, with their extensions into the biological and personal fields; if, that is to say, it referred only to those empirical investigations which employ the method of mathematical analysis. So many misunderstandings would have been avoided! For there is a persistent tendency to make general statements about "Science," whose proper reference is to the basic physical sciences only. At any rate, so far are the sciences from showing a tendency to combine towards one ultimate mathematical formulation that they multiply continually by fission.

At this point we ought to consider the place of mathematics in the physical sciences. What interests us is that the sciences are empirical, whereas pure mathematics is not. It requires no observation of objects or inductive generalisation. Does this mean that mathematics is subjective? I see no escape from the conclusion that a system of mathematics is an artefact, a product of human ingenuity. Yet the certainty that its operations provide and which made it for centuries the ideal of knowledge, and the control of the physical world which follows from the assumption that the material world has itself a mathematical structure, tell very heavily in the opposite direction. If we are to hold to our conviction that science is knowledge in the fullest sense, then the physical sciences, which are the most highly developed and the most fully verified of all the sciences, and in a sense the basis of all the others, must surely be the most objective of all. The clarity and the vitality that result from the hypothesis that the structure of the physical world is itself mathematical point in the same direction, as does the power of prediction which it bestows upon its exponents. I find myself therefore compelled to the conclusion that the objectivity of the physical sciences guarantees the objectivity of pure mathematics. But this carries with it an important corollary. We cannot accept the view that only empirical cognition admits of objectivity: and if mathematics is objective, there may be other instances of non-empirical cognition that are also capable of objectivity.

Another characteristic of the physical sciences which is bound up with their objectivity is the use of experiment, especially as a test of validity. The formula of experiment is as follows: If this hypothesis which suggests itself as a possible solution of my problem is valid, then if I do X the result will be Y. So I do X again and again, varying the conditions as much as possible. If the result is persistently other than Y, my hypothesis is disproved. If it is regularly Y, as I predicted, then I am right in accepting the hypothesis as objectively evidenced. It is not, as has often been pointed out, finally proved correct: but it is supported by the evidence so far as it goes. The special interest of this formulation is its relation to technology. For the doing of X, if satisfactorily resulting in Y, is, on its practical side, a technique for the production of Y. This is perhaps the most intimate evidence of the essential relation between science and technology, which I have argued elsewhere, and so shall refrain from repeating here. But we must note further that, in a successful experiment, the X and Y are shown to be events which stand in a causal relation. I mention this merely to remind us of the important role played in the physical sciences, by the concept of causality. It will come up again later.

THE BIOLOGICAL SCIENCES

I shall now turn our attention to the biological sciences, which form a special group because they are concerned to investigate the structure and behaviour of living creatures. We should first remind ourselves that organisms are also physical entities, and to that extent are part of the subject matter of the physical sciences. But then let us put this aspect aside, and confine ourselves to those characters which differentiate organisms from the inorganic world, so that they require a new set of sciences for their study.

An organism, whether simple or complex, is physically a combination of inorganic substances. But to break it up into its components is to kill it. It presents itself as a unity, and it behaves as a unity. It is a living creature, and consequently it must be understood as a unit. Its unity is of a special kind, often called an "organic unity," which might be defined as a unity of functional systems, each of which makes its own contribution to the life of the whole. It may be quite simple or highly complex, but this functional structure distinguishes the organism from every inorganic entity. For our purposes we may concentrate our attention on the higher animals, in which the potentiality of the organic is most completely developed.

A radical difference in our outlook on the world, however, results from the inclusion of organisms in it. The "world" of the physical sciences is highly abstract, consisting only of matter and energy. But when the biologist takes over, he cannot limit his field to a world of organisms, and ignore the inorganic. For these live in the inorganic world, and in necessary relation to it. The biologist's world is less abstract. It becomes "Nature" and Nature is made up of "organisms" and their "environment."

There are two functions of an organism which are general and peculiar to it — growth and reproduction. The two are closely related, especially if we use the term "growth" to include all the metabolic processes. The idea of evolution itself extends the concept of growth beyond the individual to the species, by means of variations in the genetic processes. It is worth mentioning that the conception of evolution is hypothetical, with much evidence to support it, though with the failure of the earlier belief in the inheritance of acquired characteristics, there is no convincing theory which can explain it. It is hardly satisfactory to fall back upon accident to explain what is clearly, if it happens at all, a matter of directed development.

Even more mysterious is the directed development of the fertilised egg to the stage when it is ready to be born as an independent organism. The successive stages of this growth are now known in considerable detail, but such explanations as are offered seem to me palpably inadequate, and even if they were adequate, to do no more than refer the problem back to an earlier stage.

There seems no reason to carry these random notes on the structure and functioning of organisms any further. Their purpose is to suggest the high complexity of functional differences which compose the unity of an organism, and to underline the limitations, up to date, of the advance of biological science. The question remains, how do they compose it? The general answer is that each separate function makes a necessary contribution to the life of the organism as a whole. If any fails, the organism either dies or falls sick or otherwise lives an incomplete or imperfect life. This, of course, means that each function maintains the requisite rhythm, and that a balance is established and regulated continuously between them to achieve an active harmony of all the parts of the body. A much more complicated answer could be given, but this must suffice. The use of aesthetic concepts in it is important to our consideration of biological objectivity.

But we cannot leave this part of our consideration of the sciences without setting the organism in its relation to the environment in which it lives, and which includes relations with other organisms of its own and different species, both zoological and botanical, as well as the inorganic world which contains and supports them all. The organism must find food there, as well as shelter and concealment or defence from its enemies. The more highly developed organisms are provided with means of locomotion, and with sensory capabilities to inform and guide these external activities. The behaviour of animals in relation to the world outside is clearly not random but directed activity. Biologists describe it, in general, as an "adaptation to environment," and in seeking explanations they characteristically use, not the concept of "cause and effect," but that of "stimulus and reaction." There are two other concepts which should be noted along with these, the concept of "health and sickness," and that of "animal intelligence." The first of these involves us in valuation, for an organism can be in good or bad health. It may also suffer from malformation, sickness or disease, so that some of its life processes "go wrong" or are "badly" performed. There is no ground for thinking that the afflicted organism is involved in this valuing. But certainly the biologist is, and he finds it an objective matter of primary observation.

VALUATION, PURPOSE, AND OBJECTIVITY

That animal behaviour exhibits intelligence, and in varying degrees, seems undeniable. If we watch a sheep dog handling a flock of sheep, or beavers building a dam, or a pair of long-tailed tits building a nest, we cannot but marvel at the intelligence they show. But if we have been to school with the scientists we will go on to consider how narrow and stereotyped these expressions of intelligence are, how unchanging from one individual to another of the same species, and from one generation to the next. Our conclusion then, is likely to be that they are probably all "unconscious" or "quasi-instinctive," and ultimately explicable in terms of "reaction to stimulus." In other words, when an observer, biologist or not, watches the behaviour of living creatures, in particular of those which move about their environment, he can hardly avoid the conclusion that their activity is purposive, and that in some sense, they know what they are doing. But he also finds good reasons to conclude that they do not form purposes, as we do, and set out to achieve them. There is no convincing evidence that any of them is capable of thinking. And when we find plants which catch flies for food, or discover a hunting wasp which performs delicate surgical operations of stinging its insect prey in its three ganglionic centres to provide fresh food for its eggs when they hatch out, we feel quite sure we are correct. Yet it remains a natural fact that organic behaviour is purposive; it is directed to ends which are normally achieved. Yet the organisms which undergo it have no purposes. We may talk about "purposiveness without a purpose" or with Aristotle about "ends without the image of the end." And no doubt there is a measure of enlightenment to be gained from such phrases, but the light is not very bright. We must, I think, admit that there is still a good deal of mystery about the life processes; and even biologists find it difficult, unless they are very careful, to avoid falling into anthropomorphisms. It is perhaps one step worse when we, or they, ascribe the purposes behind this patent purposiveness to Nature!

What then can we conclude about objectivity in the biological sciences, excluding for reasons already discussed the use of chemical and physical investigation into the nature of organisms as physical objects? We should note however that in this field organic chemistry and physics have made important discoveries which are likely to help towards the solution of strictly biological problems; and in this field objectivity is of the same type as in their primary investigation of the inorganic world. When we look at biology proper, we cannot be so sure. Of one thing there can be no doubt; the biologist is as much of a scientist as the physicist. The intention that originates and the attitude of mind that sustains his research are just as thoroughly objective. His procedure is impeccably empirical. But he has a much harder furrow to plough. His material is much more complex and variable. It is not merely subject to change, it initiates change, in itself and in other things. He must accept as he finds it any organism, from a bacillus to an elephant, as a unit because it behaves as one; to disentangle the inner structure, the organs and systems and functions by which and in which it lives, and seek for a hypothesis that will explain all this, and provide empirical evidence that will prove convincing to his fellow biologists. And this is only the beginning. But it must suffice, even if it fails to consider the vast extension brought about by the general acceptance of the theory of evolution and its consequences.

We have noticed the use of concepts drawn from aesthetic experience such as rhythm, balance and harmony in the explication of organic unity. The conception of a "balance of Nature" is an extension of the same tendency. I stress this, on what may seem a minimum of evidence, because the question of the relation of our knowledge of the organic to our own organic life would take us outside the limits of this paper, and calls for elaborate treatment, and particularly of the development of philosophy in Germany from Lessing to Hegel, in which the two themes of Nature and Art are interwoven. Its importance in the present context lies in its bearing on the objectivity of biological science. We were driven to consider pure mathematics objective because of its essential use in physical science. If art is essential to biology in a similar fashion, it raises the question of objectivity in aesthetic experence. We shall have an opportunity to refer to this later.

We have also noted that the biologist is involved in activities of valuation. The phenomena of disease and other sorts of failure in the life processes, and perhaps of death itself, provide instances of valuation which are undoubtedly objective. The existence of medical biology, and of medical science in general is satisfactory evidence for this. I have already indicated my belief that science is essentially linked with technology. The major technologies to which biological science is related are plant and animal breeding and veterinary science and in consequence these fields provide the major possibility of biological experiment. The limitations and the difficulty of experiment in these fields are well known. The cultivation of plants and the breeding of animals are apt to be slow and uncertain processes, particularly in the interpretation of results. Progress is therefore slower and less certain than in the physical sciences, though there are outstanding successes, such as the theory of bacterial infection. But we must admit that there are more recognised yet unsolved problems in biology than in the physical sciences, and that the difficulty of verification is often so great that we have to be content with a minimum of reliable evidence, or even to fall back on intelligent guess-work. So it seems undeniable that the level of objectivity in biology is considerably lower than in the physical sciences. On the other hand, achievements in descriptive biology are remarkable and highly objective.

THE PERSONAL SCIENCES

We have still to consider the human sciences, or, as I should prefer to call them, the personal sciences. My reason for this preference is that the term "human" tends to carry a biological reference; and I am concerned to stress the difference of these scie·ces from biology. The oldest is economics, probably because it lends itself to mathematical elaboration. The others are even younger, and still engaged in finding their feet. Yet where we might have expected a single science of human behaviour, we are actually faced with a proliferation of specialism, as if each aspect of human behaviour required a special science of its own.

This is one difference from biology to be noted. But there are many more important differences dictated by the nature of our subject matter on which to concentrate our attention. The central science in the field is certainly psychology, which was demanded from the early days of physical enquiry as a necessary complement to the science of matter, understood in terms of the dichotomy of matter and mind. But all efforts to found a science of mind proved fruitless, and psychology was at last established almost in our own day as the science of human behaviour — with social psychology as one of its branches, now challenged by sociology as an independent science with a somewhat different origin. I propose, therefore, to confine my attention largely to psychology.

The first clear difference between the personal sciences and all the others is the reflection of science back upon itself. Since scientific activity is part of human behaviour, it becomes part of the subject matter of science. Consequently, any general theory of human behaviour must be capable of accounting for the production of science, if it is not to be self-refuting. We must recognize, of course, that since we are organisms, there is an important place in the study of our behaviour for a human biology. But if all our activities were explicable in terms of reaction to stimulus there could be no science. Objectivity would be ruled out. Psychology and sociology cannot be departments of biology, though the early tendency to take over biological concepts uncritically is still operative. But it is on the wane, and we have got rid, for the most part, of the use of the concept of "instincts" in the human field. What corresponds to "instinct" in human behaviour is "habit." The difference is that a habit has to be learned, and consequently can be unlearned.

Perhaps the most important difference between organic and personal behaviour is that we live by knowledge, and in consequence are capable of action. Reaction to stimulus gives place to action from knowledge. There is, first, the knowledge of values which enables us to choose between possible ends. There is, secondly, knowledge of means, which enables us to achieve the ends we have chosen. Science is the deliberate enlargement and improvement of this knowledge. There is a third type of knowledge, our knowledge of one another, which is important to action, since human action is so largely cooperative. If anyone doubts the interrelation of science and technology which I have implied above, he might study the part played during the last century, in the development of theoretical physics, by the effort to invent a really efficient steam engine.

KNOWLEDGE AND ACTION

The knowledge which makes action possible includes all three types. We might call it knowledge of the situation. Action is the realization of an intention. Knowledge of the situation is objective, which, we know, does not imply certainty. It enables the agent to form an intention which is suitable to the situation, and to act for its realisation. Such action is objective. It is not the following of an impulse or the satisfaction of a desire. The agent is not doing what he wants to do. He is doing what the objective situation requires.

One characteristic of human action that is peculiar to it is that it is problematic. By this I mean that when we act we are aware that we may do the wrong thing, that when we think we know that we risk falling into error. Sensible people take precautions against these risks, and make allowances for them. But they cannot be wholly eliminated, if only because the evidence that would correct our judgment is not always available, or because our control over our means of achievement is never complete. So the contrasts of opposites such as good and bad, right and wrong, true and false, satisfactory and unsatisfactory belong of necessity to the judgment of human activity, and they are, in principle, objective. The failure of an action is evidenced by the contrast between its intention and its result.

The problematic of action greatly enlarges the field of value judgments that we have already found present in the study of organisms through the phenomena of health and disease. So a note on the objectivity of value judgments in general may be useful at this point. The view that all value judgments are subjective is certainly false. There is nothing subjective about the positive valuation of health. Tools have functions, and some perform their function better than others. A house may be badly built; a suit badly tailored. In such cases there are objective criteria for judgment.

These cases, one may object, are purely technical. In non-technical types of action there can be strong differences of opinion, and no way of deciding who is right. Certainly there are cases where our judgments are matters of taste, and in such cases the question of validity does not arise. One man's meat is another man's poison. But there are other fields where the claim to objective validity is clear, and the proof of validity is seemingly impossible. Here we must recall that we have already seen that in supporting the validity of science we are committed to the view that knowledge does not imply certainty. Differences of judgment do not prove that objectivity is impossible. We often do silly things, and realize later by their results how silly they were. To deny the objectivity of moral judgment is to deny the distinction between wisdom and stupidity. Moreover it is possible to do something because I think it right, and not because I want to do it. In that case my attitude as an agent is objective, even if my judgment of what is right is faulty. To this I should only like to add that there are necessary ends in human life, of which one is cooperation. There are also conditions of cooperation, and these provide objective grounds for moral valuation. But this must suffice on a subject that would need a paper to itself.

OBJECTIVITY AND FREUDIAN PSYCHOLOGY

To return to our special subject. Science cannot provide a full account or a full explanation of the personal. Any science presupposes the deterministic character of its subject matter, either through cause and effect, in the physical field, or through stimulus and reaction in the biological. But a person, acting from knowledge, is a determiner. To hold that all personal activity is determined, in the scientific sense, is to deny the possibility of action, and to make objectivity meaningless. There is then no room for a distinction between true and false.

It follows that psychology, as the science of human behaviour, must limit itself, consciously or unconsciously, to an aspect of human behaviour, that is to say, to what is in fact determined, but not by the agent himself. In experimental psychology, for instance, the psychologist must instruct his subject to behave in a certain fashion, and record what happens. But then he is not studying free human behaviour, but behaviour dictated by the experimenter. In this way, he may discover the reaction time of his subject, or some other element in his behaviour of which he himself is unaware. But the most effective condition for scientific investigation is in the case of mental illness. For the mark of mental illness is the inability of the patient to control his own behaviour in some respect. It has become compulsive. At once it becomes possible and necessary to seek a determinant of the compulsion; and to cure the illness is to restore his full normal control of his own actions. We need not be surprised, therefore, that it is in the field of medical psychology that the major scientific discoveries have been made. So I propose, for my purpose, to confine my remarks to the work of Freud and his successors. In passing we may note that the study of that in human behaviour which is not determined belongs to philosophy.

Freud had an unshakable faith in science. His mind was fertile and inventive, but neither profound nor critical. He dismissed religion as illusion, though the ground of this judgment could have been used as easily — and as fallaciously — against science itself. Perhaps it was as a result of both these attitudes — and more important than either — that he was able to avoid or overcome the deep and agelong subjective resistances which prevented an objective investigation of fundamental human motivation, particularly in the sexual field. He discovered "the unconscious," that is to say, those elements in ourselves, of which we are unaware, which control or influence our behaviour. He invented a method of exploring the unconscious through the interpretation of dreams and free association. He held the reductionist view that what he was dealing with in these explorations were forces in active tension with one another, and which ought to and eventually would be formulated mathematically. In the meantime, for the use of himself and others, he built a mythology of the unconscious, partly derived from ancient mythologies — "the Oedipus Complex," for instance — and partly from metaphor, like "the Censor." In what sense, if any, can this mythology properly be called "objective"? In the first place, the attitude of mind of the psychiatrist is as objective as that of any other scientist. The theory he accepts and uses as a methodology of healing is the result of observation and experience, though these, in the nature of the case, are indirect. It is also open to the critical judgment of all other qualified psychiatrists. Such criticism has not been lacking and has led to modifications and extensions of the mythology. But the hope of a mathematical analysis of psychic forces has made no headway and remains a wild hope. More to the point is the observation that as biology finds help in conceiving and describing the unity of the organic in the activities of art, so the description of the structure and content of the "unconscious" points in the direction of religion, which is the major source of mythology. The reason may well be that both are concerned with personal relations, and both find themselves constrained to use the language of sensory experience to refer in a meaningful fashion to what transcends and yet is related to ordinary conscious experience. The use of mythology in the personal sciences, however, is not confined to medical psychology. Economics has its "economic man," and anthropologists, from the study of a few bones, will sketch for us the living appearance of human creatures long extinct.

SUMMING UP

Finally, a summing up seems required, though I should be happy to leave it to the reader. I shall make my own as concise as possible. The basic issue, with which I began, was this. If we are to accept the results of science as knowledge in the full sense, as I think we must, then we must agree that knowledge does not imply certainty. It does, however — and I hope the reader will agree — imply objectivity. I have rejected, as not merely erroneous but ridiculous, the belief that science has a monopoly of objectivity, and so of knowledge in the full sense. I was concerned to suggest that science is itself limited, as the essential connection between pure science and technology indicates.

I chose to consider different branches of science, to show that there is no Science in general, and that the method any science employs, and the concepts it uses, are in large part dictated by its subject matter. All sciences are empirical, and this means that we cannot assume, without loss of objectivity, that concepts and methods that are applicable in one field will be applicable in another. The problems to be solved must be set by the character of the field of investigation. Cause-and-effect becomes in biology stimulus-and-reaction, and in the human field, knowledge-and-action.

The sciences refer us beyond themselves. They all are rooted in the traditional knowledge which we call common sense. Its elements are not certain, and they are not the result of activities which are aimed at knowledge. But they are tested in experience, and unless they largely worked in practice they would soon be discarded. Since they are produced in action and tested in action, and since they are generally agreed upon and subjected to continuous questioning, they have at least some claim to objectivity. They are not certain, but knowledge does not imply certainty, so their claim to constitute a common knowledge may be admitted. A good part of science has consisted in the clarification and extension, or the criticism and refutation, of this common knowledge.

But, as we have seen, different sciences refer us also to non-scientific types of reflective experience — physical science to pure mathematics on which it is so largely dependent, biological science to aesthetic experience, and personal science to religion. This raises the question whether these forms of experience are not potentially objective. It would be at best very odd to deny objectivity to pure mathematics, which comes nearer to providing certainty than any other mode of reflection, even more than pure logic. All tunes and all paintings are not works of art. I suggest that those which are, are so by virtue of an objectivity of their own, which is a product of their own form of reflection, a search, always serious and sometimes desperate, for the adequate expression of an image. Moreover the arts of language, such as literature and drama, form major sources of our knowledge of human life and human behaviour. It is a little ridiculous to deny them their standing as knowledge, even if we must admit that it is perhaps knowledge of the possible rather than the actual. It might be interesting to note that the early cubist painters insisted that they were throwing overboard the falsities of convention and seeking to grasp and express reality. As for religion, I would add only two things. First, that the outstanding religious leaders of the world have been marked by an understanding of human nature and human society that has stood the test of centuries. The other is that in public discussions of important issues, it is apt to be theologians, rather than scientists or even philosophers, who impress one by their depth of insight.

I suppose I must conclude with an expression of how I think this study of the sciences bears upon the question of objectivity. What *is* objectivity? Is it a character of what is known, or of the knowing of it? Probably both: we found ourselves, at least, required to use it in both applications. But the application which remains constant throughout the variety of sciences we looked at was the objective attitude of mind. It is the state of mind that makes science possible, sustaining the readiness to abandon a cherished belief when the evidence turns against it; it is the demand that the search for adequate evidence be carried through, the submission of conclusions and their evidence to the critical judgment of a community of scientists, and so forth. But these are rather concomitants and consignments than characters of objectivity. What they manifest or ensure is that the centre of interest in the activity of cognition is in the *object* and not in the self that cognises it. If I am right in thinking that this is the core of objectivity, then I should go farther and say that it is the expression, in the field of cognition, of the capacity for self-transcendence. Or as William Davis, himself a theologian, has phrased it, it is "the ability to direct one's awareness away from oneself."

Science, Metaphysics, and Teleology/

ERROL E. HARRIS

Among the majority of scientists and philosophers today teleology is largely taboo. A teleological account or explanation of evolution, of biological form, of physiological function (that term notwithstanding) or of animal behaviour is at once taken as the hallmark of unscientific mystery-mongering, whether the form of teleology implied is theistic, vitalistic or simply holistic. If this rejection is well founded it must be based upon some alternative, and presumably more reliable, conception of the nature of things, and one which is in itself more intelligible. I propose, therefore, to examine some alternative possibilities to a teleological view of the world in general to see if they can satisfy these requirements. That a teleological view is metaphysical, most of its critics declare and many of its advocates would admit. But that the alternatives are also metaphysical theories may be an unpalatable fact to many who oppose teleology. Unfortunately for them, it is an inescapable fact, because as I have said a universal exclusion of teleology must be based upon the affirmation of some general character of things. If teleological explanation involves one kind of metaphysical view, it can be opposed or disproved only on the ground, acknowledged or latent, of some other metaphysical theory: recent attempts to ignore and evade this fact have resulted only in indefensible dogmatism.

Metaphysics, by its very nature, attributes to the world at large one or more general characteristics of a universally pervasive kind, and metaphysical systems which place the ultimate principle of explanation in final causes, more especially in some one ultimate final cause, are rightly described as teleological. Some systems, like Aristotle's or Hegel's, attribute a teleological character to everything in the universe and to the universe as a whole; but it is possible to conceive of a theory which does not take the world in general to have this character. This would be a theory which does not hold that the world can be understood only in terms of ideals or ends at which its processes aim or to which they tend, while it nevertheless countenances the possibility that some processes in the world may have that character.

A view of the world which tolerates teleological explanation in some cases but does not require it in all would be obliged, in order to be consistent and coherent, to provide some explanation of the possibility and occurrence of the difference between non-teleological and teleological processes. It would be faced with the question how, in a non-teleological setting, teleological processes could arise.

The undeniable facts which must be accounted for are, first, human reflective awareness, and second, the consequent possibility both of orderly and systematic knowledge of the world, and of organized purposive behavior. The last two are forms of activity which discover structure in, or impose it upon the environment in which man lives and upon his experience of it. They are undeniable because any denial must be self-refuting. Significantly to deny the existence of reflective awareness (as Descartes showed) one must be reflectively aware. In order to deny the existence of orderly and systematic knowledge with any degree of credibility one must possess some orderly and systematic knowledge on which to base the denial. To deny the occurrence of purposive behavior is itself to perform a purposive act. The phenomena of human experience are thus key facts which any view of the world must accommodate and, if it is to be intelligible, must satisfactorily explain.

A mixed view tolerating both teleological and non-teleological processes tends when pressed to revert to one of the other two;

for unless it appeals to teleological principles to explain the non-teleological or else reduces the teleological processes to non-teleological ones, it is forced to maintain a radical dualism. Any attempt to account for interrelation and interaction between the two types of process then brings the consistency of the theory into jeopardy.

Consequenly the rejection of teleology is liable to be whole-hearted, with the explanation of everything including human mentality attempted by other than final causes. Such a theory is committed to a reduction of all processes to some non-teleological form, including any kind of evolution or development, any apparently purposive behavior and even human subjectivity itself. Doctrines of this kind are physicalistic, commonly mechanistic in some significant sense, and atheistic—for clearly the introduction of God as creator or director of mundane events would be a new infiltration of teleology.

It is the latter type of theory which I intend first to examine. I shall not criticize the work of any individual philosopher, but shall consider what may be (and usually is) held by anyone who resolutely sets himself to exclude from his theory any form of teleology, and I shall try to show that this cannot consistently be done. I shall then give some attention to the alternative and outline briefly its salient characteristics.

Non-Teleological Metaphysics

The doctrine known as physicalism maintains that all events without exception can in the last resort be accurately described in the language of physical science. As the term was originally used by Carnap and the Vienna Circle it was intended to refer only to semantic analysis and was not supposed to have any metaphysical implications, but it is clear that if language bears significant relation to its referent, metaphysical implications are unavoidable. The obvious effect of the doctrines is to foster belief in a reality which is purely material, in which all events obey the laws of physics exclusively and which can be fully and satisfactorily explained by those laws.

Further, if teleology is to be rigidly rejected, the laws of physics cannot be regarded as laws of order and system for there must be no immanent principle of organization in the nature of things. Any such principle would work teleologically for it would have to be one which systematically brought into existence orderly arrangements of elements where none had previously existed. The laws of physics must therefore be taken as statistical laws defining the probability of specific events and concomitances under specified initial conditions.

Primordial physical processes would have to be some sort of purely random movement of particles or energy exchanges and any semblance of order or structure would arise by chance in the course of the primordial random activity. Thus physical laws would be probability laws stating the mathematical relationships between these chance events.

In a world of this nature orderly structures occurring by chance would persist if circumstances permitted but would disintegrate if the random changes were such as make their survival impossible. Any accidental structure which happened to include an arrangement resistant to dissolution would have relatively superior survival value and would be "naturally selected." Further chance complications in structures selected in this way could increase their survival value, and so more complex and "better adapted" entities would progressively come into being, in an evolutionary sequence based entirely on chance variation and natural selection. In this way, the entire range of natural forms which we observe would have come into being, from the starry heavens to living organisms including conscious, thinking, theorizing scientists.

The reduction by scientists of living processes to chemistry and physics is well advanced and apparently supports a view such as the physicalist one I am outlining. Neo-darwinism—the view of biological evolution as involving nothing besides chance mutation and natural selection—is widespread among biologists. Behaviorism, which discounts introspective descriptions of consciousness and claims to account for so-called conscious activity solely by reference to publicly observable events (waiving any question about the nature of "public observation" itself) is a further manifestation of the same metaphysical but non-teleological tendency; and associated with it is the enterprise of constructing purely mechanical theories of purposive behavior by means of cybernetics and servo-mechanisms, and of thinking on the principles governing electronic and other forms of mechanical computers.

I shall not be concerned here to discuss the degree of success or failure with which these attempts have met,[1] but shall draw attention only to certain general considerations which seem to be fatal to the whole position.

What we have so far been reviewing is a range of entities of increasingly complex structure and behavior involving progressive advance in organization and mutually adjusted variety of form. The degree of this complexity and the intricacy and nicety of the adjustment in living organisms becomes prodigious to the point of incalculability. But the fundamental assumption of the entire metaphysical outlook of physicalism is that everything occurs in accordance with physical laws which are statistical, and where statistical laws apply the overriding principle of activity is the Second Law of Thermodynamics, according to which, in any closed system entropy, or disorder, continuously increases. It is assumed that all activity is primarily random movement, and where random movement prevails, the occurrence of any non-random arrangement is improbable. The improbability increases with the degree of order and increases exponentially as any series of events successively enhancing orderly structure continues.

The universe is, more or less by its definition and nature as the total sum of physical reality, a closed system,[2] and the account which contemporary science gives of its history is throughout evolutionary—the story of progressive increase of order and complication. Doubt is no longer cast upon the assumption of biological evolution: nowadays it is as confidently assumed that living forms originate from non-living ones in a continuous process. But the Second Law of Thermodynamics should make all this virtually impossible.

According to that law, the emergence of ordered wholes from the chaos of random movement should be rare, and the probability of stable arrangements should always be low. If stable arrangement should ever occur its modification in the direction of greater stability or more orderly complexity would be even more improbable than its occurrence. In point of fact, when we come to living things we find stability sacrificed to adaptability, a state of affairs statistically improbable beyond belief. Thus the whole conception of a purely physical universe subject to statistical laws but including evolutionary series of events generating increasingly complex orders is incoherent and self-contradictory — or at the very best incredibly improbable.

Arguments may be offered, however, in attempts to mitigate this judgment. It may be said that the improbability of evolution is lessened by natural selection, for once forms with survival value have emerged and accumulate there is a greater probability that one of them may change in the evolutionary direction. But first of all, the accumulation of ordered structures is itself highly improbable. Secondly, natural selection is strictly speaking an inapplicable term except with respect to self-reproducing structures subject to mutations. For what is not a structure has no clear individuality to preserve, and what does not reproduce itself either persists or disintegrates: in neither case is it "selected" in any intelligible sense. On the other hand self-replication by a system is an event of stupendous improbability presupposing a whole train of improbable events at the inorganic level. Thirdly, if this objection is waived, natural selection, even if assumed to take place, cannot increase the probability of any kind of variation, because it has no positive effect. Changes occur (so it is presumed) by chance; if they have survival value then the changed entity is more likely to survive, but the entity does not become more variable in any manner either favorable or unfavorable to further survival. In a highly complicated and already unstable living organism, a change increasing survival value is always far less probable than the opposite. Natural selection is not a positive influence; nothing is selected by it; what cannot survive is simply eliminated. The probability of evolutionary advance is therefore not increased by natural selection.

Nevertheless, it may be argued that however improbable long evolutionary progressions may be, given sufficient time they may still occur in an assemblage of randomly moving particles which is sufficiently large. But contemporary physics has determined, by an impressive body of mutually corroborative evidence, definite limits both to the extent and to the age of the physical universe, such that neither is sufficient to accommodate the degree of improbability involved in the evolution of living forms.

But a more serious objection than any of these arises, and it is fatal to the basic assumption of the whole metaphysical position in question. This is the assumption of the primordial occurrence of random activity—activity which, like all movement, is conceivable only if there is some kind of particle or element of which the motion can be random. Moreover, a physicalist metaphysics assumes some order or arrangement that is randomized. This idea could reasonably have been conceived in the nineteenth century, when physicists thought of atoms as hard impenetrable spheres of matter moving about in space independently of any energy system. It could also be assumed by the kinetic theory of gases, where one is dealing with large but definitely denumerable assemblages of molecules within a confined space. But contemporary physics knows nothing of elementary particles prior to the existence of energy systems upon which the particles depend both for their existence and for their motion. Even free-moving particles attached to no group, like neutrons expelled from atoms under bombardment, are held to be wave packets or energy-structures dependent for their being and nature on wider energy systems. As soon as one speaks of waves one is committed to the notion of periodicity and ordered structure, for that is precisely what a wave is. If then order and system of some sort are, in the very nature of matter, prior to the existence of distinguishable particles, it cannot be the case that order and system arise only by chance as a result of the random movement of pre-existing particles.

The exclusion of teleology from our account of the world, however, forbids the admission of order and system as a necessary product of physical activity. If it occurs of necessity, as the result of an ordering principle inherent in the nature of things, the process is teleological. In that case it is not possible to found a non-teleological metaphysic on the presumption that all events obey the laws of physics, if the laws of physics are to be those currently accepted by scientists.

The anti-teleologist may, nevertheless, think that he has an avenue of escape, though it involves a somewhat drastic renunciation on the part of the scientist. Our science, he may say, which discovers structure and order in the most elementary physical matrix, discovers only what the nature of our thinking imposes on its subject matter. In order to understand the world we experience we must impose upon it some principles of order and all our science is the outcome of such imposition. What the actual nature of the world is we do not and cannot know, and it does not follow from the fact that our science reveals structure and evolution in the world that the world is teleologically ordered. Kant, who adopted this sort of theory, left it an open question whether things in themselves did after all constitute a teleological system; but modern philosophers who hold comparable views seem ready to assert more dogmatically that the real is no more than a random succession of particular events without any systematic order, but that science imposes an order upon it such as will make our experience of these bare particulars intelligible.

Possibly my statement of this position is more crude than any exponent of it would tolerate, or perhaps I have just misunderstood those I think to be exponents, and really there are none. If so the view is simply an Aunt Sally that I have invented, and no harm will be done by demolishing her; for, surely, this theory is most incoherent. If our minds impose order upon an experience which is really an experience of chaos, our science must be a texture of illusion and it is hard to see how any such spurious ordering would enable us to act successfully in a really chaotic world. But let us not be too captious. Perhaps to be consistent we should hold that our experience of our own action is similarly illusory and that we live in a perpetual dream of order and purpose.

Even that however is an inconsistent presumption. For what we cannot deny is that we do experience a world and that it is within tolerable limits systematic and orderly, and our science, so far as it achieves its aim of understanding, subjects it to more rigorous ordering. Similarly in our practical life, so far as we act intelligently, we act in an orderly and systematic manner and strive to organize our relations with our environment, natural and human. Accordingly, our intelligent activity is systematic. But we ourselves and our activity, practical and intellectual, are part of the world. If the world by nature and in essence is chaotic, if it consists merely of a random succession of bare particulars, how do intelligent, organizing beings come to be part of it? They could not evolve out of something totally random, for what does not contain within it the conditions of systematic activity cannot produce systematic activity out of itself. And if it could there would be evolution in the world from chaos to order, and that would imply the operation of some teleological principle, running counter to the Second Law of Thermodynamics.

The only remaining possibility is to hold that our minds are totally other than and different from the material world, and do not belong to it. But if we embrace this, we shall have to maintain so stark a dualism that we shall be hard put to understand what sort of relation could exist between our minds and our bodies. Either they could not both belong to the same world and thus could hardly belong to one another, and what sort of interrelation or interaction between them would be possible would be an inscrutable mystery. Or what appear to us as our bodies must be figments of our own imaginations which do not in the least correspond to the real material entities to which our minds are somehow supposed to be attached. Similarly the relation between the material world and our minds would become totally unintelligible: what we know as the material world would be simply another figment. We should then be engulfed in Berkeleyan idealism and descend the slippery slope into solipsism, the ultimate abysm of incoherence. But this is a sorry denouement for an attempt to account in a physicalist and non-teleological theory for the orderly operation of our own intellects.

Teleological Metaphysics

Throughout the foregoing discussion I have used the word teleology in what some may think too wide a sense, for I have included as "teleological" any active principle or process which creates order out of relative disorder, or as our communication engineers would say, extracts message from noise—any process, in fact, which reduces entropy or increases information (in the literal sense of imposing form upon the unformed). Despite etymology, I believe this to be the legitimate sense in which to use the world "teleology" for—even though "telos" means "end" and we generally restrict the term "teleological" to processes which tend toward some preconceived end or goal-state—goal-seeking processes are only special cases of informed or informing behavior. What actively seeks a goal acts in accordance with a plan or rule of behavior; and rule implies order and system. Conscious purpose, which is the paradigm case of teleological activity, is explicitly action in accordance with a plan, or by design. It is variable action that adapts itself to circumstances in a systematic fashion in order to reach its end, which is not necessarily its final stage, but which does involve the completion of some pattern of activity. It is this systematic and orderly character of our own conscious life which no metaphysical theory can overlook, if only because it is involved in the very attempt to excogitate a metaphysical theory. This is true of even an anti-systematic metaphysic like Existentialism, for a philosopher who reflects upon his experience and finds it absurd must use some criterion of rationality by which to condemn it. If he then adopts a theory of life and action which enables him, as a philosopher, to accept and reconcile himself to the absurd, or to overcome and transcend it, he does so in virtue of and by means of his rational capacity. Existentialism, in fact, by its refusal to surrender subjectivity to an external and objective analysis, is insisting upon the very point I am trying to make in this paper—that human conscious existence must be taken into account by any metaphysic and that no metaphysic which fails to accommodate it can stand. This failure is typical of all non-teleological metaphysics because it excludes from the fundamental nature of things any active principle of orderly creation.

It follows that a consistent and successful metaphysics has to be teleological. The metaphysician must expect to find some positive principle at work in the world which creates order, increases information and reduces chaos or "noise," and he must expect this because in its absence there could be no thinker in the world to seek philosophical comprehension of the nature of things and so no metaphysician. This is an a priori reason for expecting the world to be teleological, and a sound one. But science provides us with empirical evidence and empirical reasons for maintaining that there must be some teleological principle operative in the nature of things. It tells us that random activity increases entropy and that long evolutionary processes are too improbable to be accidental; and it also tells us that they occur. It discovers besides that elementary particles are not so much particulate as features of an energy system; and, if we are to accept Schroedinger's arguments, they are like gestalten or relatively persistent patterns imposed on an underlying flux of wave-motion. In short, they appear as information. If this be so, the fundamental assumption even of physics must be the existence of system, and random activity can be conceived only in relation to some form of order.

Prima facie, order might be imposed upon the world in either of two ways. It might be complete from the start and all-pervasive, or it might appear germinally in a chaotic matrix and realize itself progressively through an evolutionary process. These alternatives, however, are only apparent, for each requires and implies the other.

That evolution can begin germinally within a chaotic matrix is a possibility we have already rejected, unless we could assume the introduction of order from some outside source. Even then we should be hard put to explain its maintenance and augmentation without assuming some extraneous influence and control. But there is no source outside of, and nothing extraneous to, the universe as a whole. Therefore any evolutionary account must somehow accommodate the conception of an all-pervasive order.

Order necessarily implies wholeness, for no pattern, structure or system can be incomplete and partial in principle. The very concepts of incompleteness and partiality imply a whole to which the part belongs and which completes the unfinished fragment. Even a continuous series, like the series of natural numbers, which, though ordered in regular sequence, is endless, may be regarded as a totality or set, as in Cantor's conception of transfinite numbers. The order of such a series consists in its being generated according to a precise rule. But this is not the paradigm case of order, in the sense of system, which requires structure, as it were, in depth, and a self-closure which precludes endless progression.

The progressive realization of order therefore implies the existence (in some sense)—the subsistence or at least the projection in idea—of the totality which is being progressively realized and in principle constitutes the consummation of the process. The projection of the totality in idea presupposes an already high degree of realization; for only a thinker could conceive such a whole, and a thinker is a highly developed, highly complex and integrated organism, performing an activity of ordering and structuring at an advanced level of coherence. What is being projected, therefore, is something already to a great extent realized, and the projection is possible only in virtue of that realization and as a continuation of the process. Thus Descartes could argue that to have the idea of a perfect being implies a cause of the idea which already contains "formally" or "eminently" as much reality as the idea contains "objectively."

The process, moreover, is teleological—one in which the operative principle of progression must be a nisus to wholeness. If it were not, the progressive realization of order would be accidental and that we have found to be impossible. Reality in some form, therefore, cannot be denied to that whole the ordering principle of which is actually operative in the process of generation, just as it is impossible to deny the existence of order prior to that of elementary particles, if they are products of energy systems. As the process is teleological it can be fully understood and explained only in the light of its completion. Thus unless the totality is in some sense real nothing would be intelligible. It is, moreover, not enough to call it simply potential, for what is potentially present is also in some sense actually present, though it is exceedingly difficult to say in what sense. As potential it is not actualized, in Aristotle's sense of *energeia,* but it is nevertheless present in potency in the process of actualization, and that is as much as to say that the actualized form is in some way operative (potent) from the start. To call it potential is to call it *partially* actual; but that is no more than by implication to claim reality for that whole of which it is the partial realization. The progressive evolution of a whole posits the reality of the form of the realized whole.

But, it may be asked, how can all-pervasive order permit of an evolutionary progression from greater to less disorderliness? A totally ordered universe has no room for evolution; it would be, like the Substance of Spinoza, a fixed and eternal totality devoid of all process, or one in which any process or movement would be only an appearance—or an "inadequate idea." I shall attempt to show in brief compass that any such belief is the opposite of the truth and that an all-inclusive order is one which must and can only reveal itself seriatim in a succession of forms progressively more adequate to the perfection of the completed whole.

If the universe is identified with the ordered totality, as it is by Spinoza, the exclusion of dialectical progression is only apparent (this fact, as I have tried to show elsewhere,[3] reveals itself in Spinoza's system). The totality cannot manifest itself as a whole in any one point, or any one moment of time, nor can it be understood as a whole (in all detail) in any one judgment. Both it and the knowledge of it must, therefore, in order to be complete, unfold itself as a series or growth. Any part, or element, or phase, insofar as it is a part of the whole, is incomplete and inadequate, yet equally it implies the totality and so contains it potentially and is a germ of the whole from which the development can proceed. The totality is thus at once immanent in the part and transcendent beyond it. Further, it is transcendent beyond any mere sum or assemblage of parts so far as it is the manifestation of an organizing principle which constitutes the whole into a gestalt or form, and which is not realized in anything short of the consummated totality; just as the collection of lines and the colors which make up a pattern is something less than and is not the pattern as such, or the collection of parts and chemical processes which make up an organism are not, and are transcended by, the life of the organic unity.

We come closer to the correct conception of such a system or ordered totality when we realize that it is not, and in the nature of the case, could not be, a static quasi-spatial pattern, but is a process or activity proceeding dialectically from less to more complex forms of organized unity. The antithetical alternatives I have been discussing turn out to be opposite or contrasting aspects of the same thing. An evolutionary series taken as a whole is an organic system, as is the growth of a germ cell into a mature animal; and an organic totality revealing itself in time always does so as the dialectical generation of system. Each stage in the development is both a prefiguring of the ultimate totality with a specific degree of adequacy to its fully developed character,[4] and, as a specific stage of development implies, through its relations to them, the other phases of the process. However low in the scale we descend we never reach zero, for there is no zero in the scale. "In order to be anything, it is necessary to begin by being something." As each phase is implicitly what is throughout coming to fulfilment, the whole is always immanent. As the development proceeds nothing is lost and something is continually gained, so that at every stage the prior process is summed and preserved as well as (relatively) fulfilled and transcended. Consequently, the final phase must be, at once "the end" transcendent beyond anything anterior to it in the process, and the entire process itself—the system or totality which is both a whole and one with the process. It must be transcendently and eternally whole, yet everlastingly self-realizing. Thus, though it may be wholly or partially manifested in and as a temporal process, it is not itself temporal, but transcends all temporal series. Even so, its logical structure is that of a dialectical scale in which, to quote F. H. Bradley, "Every part is in the whole and determines that whole . . . the whole is in every part, and informs each part with the nature of the whole."

All this can be (and often is) alternatively expressed in the religious language of theism. God is the all-embracing *Ens Realissimum* in whom everything lives and moves and has its being. He is the source, the ground, and the creative principle of all things, immanent in all things and transcendent beyond all things—eternally real, eternally active and everlastingly self-manifesting and self-realizing in the world.

Intelligent thinking, which we are conscious of exercising in our own experience and which enables us, so far as we do, to make sense of the world about us, is an activity of ordering and structuring. It has often been argued that its procedure as well as its products are dialectical in character and, were sufficient time and space at our disposal, that might here be demonstrated and exemplified. But I need not go to such lengths so long as the truth of the opening statement of this paragraph is admitted. Our thinking, as we consciously perform it, therefore, presents us with systems; and, however incomplete they may prove to be, each by itself and all taken together constitute phases in such a process as has been described above. To account for it adequately, therefore, will be to account for it dialectically, as itself a scale of developing forms, and as a phase or series of phases within a larger, more inclusive scale. To account for it wholly, as belonging to the universe of which it is itself conscious, a similar account must be given of that universe, finding a place in it for our own minds and consciousnesses. Every metaphysic is committed to the task of accounting for human awareness, for the reason I have already given, that human awareness is an inescapable and undeniable fact of the world of which understanding is being sought. No metaphysic can omit it from its purview without committing the Epistemologist's Fallacy of exempting itself from its own theory of the nature of the real. And no adequate account can be given of this ineluctable fact which is not of the kind I have outlined.

The outcome of this discussion is, first, that a non-teleological metaphysic cannot be made self-consistent and ends either in incoherence or else in tacit dependence upon a teleological presupposition. And second, it is that a teleological metaphysic can be made self-consistent and coherent only if it is dialectical in character; consequently, it will turn out to be both transcendental and expressible as theism. As teleology seems to be the only viable option for the metaphysician, theism of some sort is unavoidable. Those who attempt to avoid this conclusion by renouncing metaphysics cannot do so rationally—for the only rational grounds for renouncing metaphysics must be some principle which excludes a certain type of theorizing as untrue, unmeaning, or impossible in the nature of things. Any such principle would of necessity be metaphysical, and only by metaphysics could the thesis it supports be established.

Footnotes

¹ I have paid some attention to this in my essay "Mind and Mechanical Models," in *Theories of the Mind,* ed. Jordan Scher (Chicago: The Free Press, 1962). Cf. also H. L. Dreyfus, "Why Computers Must Have Bodies in order to be Intelligent," *Review of Metaphysics* 21 (Sept., 1967):13–32; *Alchemy and Artificial Intelligence* (Santa Monica, Calif.: Rand Corp., 1965), and *What Computers Can't Do* (New York: Harper and Row, 1972).

² Recent astronomical evidence discovered by Martin Ryle has rendered the Open System of Hoyle less tenable and favors the Evolutionary Theory typified by Lemaître.

³ *Nature, Mind and Modern Science* (London: Allen and Unwin, 1954), chap. 11; *Salvation from Despair* (The Hague: Martinus Nijhoff, 1973), chap. 6, arts. 6–8.

⁴ Cf. John Macmurray, *Interpreting the Universe* (London: Faber and Faber, 1952): "Earlier stages are only stages in the process because they lead to a mature state. An organism can be defined only in terms of its maturity, and its growth only as a series of forms which it takes on in its progress to maturity" (p. 112).

No Man Is An Island . . ./

A. R. C. DUNCAN

KNOWLEDGE, ACTION, AND FRIENDSHIP

In the preface to his Gifford Lectures John Macmurray says: "The simplest expression that I can find for the thesis I have tried to maintain is this: all meaningful knowledge is for the sake of action and all meaningful action for the sake of friendship." Although this provocative statement is indeed the simplest and a most accurate account of Macmurray's philosophy, it requires interpretation. Accordingly, although in this paper I shall devote myself to clarifying the intellectual background of Macmurray's Gifford Lectures, a few general remarks about this programmatic note are first in order.

In the first place, it must be understood that for Macmurray friendship is the ideal form of relationship between persons, and hence the form of personal relation that must be examined if we are fully to understand the true nature of genuinely personal relationships. Secondly, Macmurray identifies the field of personal relations as the field of religion. If we ask what religion is about (and not as so often is asked, what is religion) [1] then Macmurray replies that religion is about personal relations. Thirdly, a genuine personal relationship cannot begin unless the persons involved do something. Friendship demands not simply that one think about one's friend, but that one should make some gesture of commitment to the other person, some act of self-revelation which must be responded to by some reciprocal act of commitment or self-revelation. Fourthly, action for Macmurray is more fundamental than thought, which is basically the negative aspect of action. Thought does not include action, but action includes thought. In his Gifford Lectures Macmurray develops a powerful argument designed to show that since Descartes the theoretical and egocentric presuppositions of traditional philosophy have prevented it from reaching satisfactory solutions to its problems. To avoid the impasse into which we have fallen, he argues that we must substitute for the Cartesian 'I think' of the subject seeking knowledge the 'I do' of the agent living in a world of things, living creatures and persons. At least as an experiment we should attempt to discover where a different set of basic presuppositions might lead us, the presuppositions of the self as agent.

Obviously Macmurray's philosophical position must stand or fall by its capacity to give a consistent and fruitful interpretation of human experience in all its aspects, scientific, moral, religious, and aesthetic. However, since Macmurray's mode of philosophising is different from that adopted by many contemporary philosophers intimidated by the twentieth century wave of positivists, I should like in this paper to indicate some of the influences and events which combined in Macmurray's thinking to lead him to the position he has adopted. Although with many philosophers there is little or no connection between their abstract metaphysical or logical thinking and their personal lives, this is not always the case and is not likely to be so with a philosopher who maintains categorically that "when philosophy is alive it grows straight out of human life" and that "academic philosophy like academic art is nearly always dead."[2] The first task of the philosopher, Macmurray holds, is to detect the right problem, the right question to ask, and "he can only do that by seeking an objective understanding of the situation in which [he] has to make [his] contribution as a philosopher to the life of his day and generation"; and that in turn means that "to be a philosopher one must know a great deal that is not philosophy, and the literary sources of any significant philosopher are by no means confined to philosophical literature. The ideas which a philosopher orders and analyses, and which in a sense form the raw material of his industry, come to him from varied sources. . . . in histories and essays, in poetry and fiction, as well as in the writings of scientists and theologians."[3] By nature, temperament, and deliberate choice Macmurray is a philosopher rather than a philosophical scholar or pure logician. He has written no studies of the thought of other philosophers, but for his raw material he has looked to social and political events in the world in which he lives and to the activities of psychologists, artists, theologians and historians. He has understood his task as a philosopher to be that of criticising unexamined assumptions and formulating a set of general ideas in terms of which human life may be understood.

Two Formative Events

Bertrand Russell once remarked that people frequently come to philosophy from a prior interest in either science or religion. There is a good deal of truth in this, but Macmurray is unusual in that he had strong prior interests in *both* religion and science. Brought up in the kind of Scottish home where religion was taken seriously, Macmurray was schooled in the classics and, despite his expressed desire to become a scientist, was persuaded to read Classics at Glasgow followed by Greats at Oxford. After one brief year at Oxford war broke out and from 1914 to 1919 Macmurray served with the British army in Flanders. Two events occurred in these years which were to affect his philosophical development. The first one can be related in his own words:

> Through the experience of war I moved a long way towards my own reality. The first, and perhaps the most effective change which the experience of the battle field worked in me, was the result of becoming familiar with death. In normal civilian life one hardly ever meets death, and when one does it is heavily disguised. For the combatant soldier it is not an idea; it is a stark, everpresent unavoidable fact. . . . No doubt this normal experience of the soldier on active service affects men differently. With me it resulted in a quick and complete acceptance of death, for myself as well as for my comrades. It had seemed a dreaded end before the war. Now it became an incident in life, and in the result it removed for ever the *fear* of death. This is a tremendous gain in reality, for until we reach it — however we do reach it — we cannot see our life as it really is, and so cannot live it as we should. The fear of death is in us the symbol of all fear; and fear is destructive of reality. . . . Without this knowledge of death, I came to believe, there can be no real knowledge of life and so no discovery of the reality of religion.[4]

The fruits of this experience are to be seen in the chapters on religion and pseudo-religion in *Creative Society* and in his insistence that not hate but fear is the destructive opposite of love, a dominant motif in his *Persons in Relation*.

The second event was his decisive break with organised religion, which came about partly because, like so many other soldiers in that first world war, he lost faith in the society for which he was allegedly fighting (though not his faith in religion) and partly because of the hostile response of a Christian congregation when, asked to preach in uniform in a London church, he advised

> the church and the Christians in it to guard against the war mentality; and to keep themselves as far as possible aloof from the quarrel so that they would be in a position — and of a temper — to undertake their proper task as Christians when the war was over of reconciliation. The congregation took it badly; I could feel a cold hostility menacing me; and no one spoke to me when the service was over. It was after this service that I decided, on Christian grounds, that I should never when the war was over remain or become a member of any Christian church. . . . I spoke thereafter and wrote in defence of religion and Christianity; but I thought of the churches as the various national religions of Europe.[5]

For a man who had at one time thought of becoming a missionary this was a grave decision but it gave him an unusual degree of freedom from institutional constraint in pursuing his philosophical study of religion.

Anxious to partake in any activity which might help to prevent a recurrence of the 1914–18 war, Macmurray thought of taking a post with the League of Nations but eventually decided that he could best make his contribution through the teaching of philosophy, thereby taking his stand with those who believe that philosophical thinking is immediately relevant to the business of living. The Oxford to which Macmurray returned after the war was dominated philosophically by the idealists and realists. Unable to accept the position of either school, Macmurray relates that he read them on alternate days seeking to identify the points on which the two schools agreed, for there, he felt, would be found those unexamined assumptions with which a philosopher should be primarily occupied. This marks him off from the contemporary type of school-philosopher who recognises as philosophically significant only those writers who share the same basic assumptions or who subscribe to whatever slogans may be currently in fashion.

PHILOSOPHY AND SCIENCE

Shortly after his return to Oxford Macmurray was present at an Oxford philosophical meeting at which the newly-appointed Professor of Physics, F.A. Lindemann, later Lord Cherwell, had been invited to talk about relativity.[6] After Lindemann had completed his address, two Oxford professors of philosophy, A.H. Smith and H.W.B. Joseph, endeavoured to show by logical demonstration that the theory of relativity was false. Their general line appears to have been that so-called scientific knowledge was not really knowledge at all because it was largely hypothetical and empirical and thus bereft of the element of certainty which, it was held, must characterise all knowledge worthy of the name. Like many of the other younger men present Macmurray found the attitude of the philosophers nothing short of ludicrous and set out to rethink for himself his philosophy of science. Starting from the position that if anything deserved the name of knowledge, then what was achieved by the natural scientist deserved the title in the highest degree, Macmurray argued that experiment was what distinguished scientific activity from either logical demonstration or any form of intuitive thought. Two of his conclusions are of importance for our present purposes. First, he pointed out that "in its proper sense experiment is practical. It involves doing things, physical things"[7] and hence it follows that "science is a method of discovery in which overt practical activity plays an essential part" or more simply "to know we must act as well as think and perceive." Secondly, he concluded that science . . . makes no claim to offer us certainty at any point. It dissolves every judgment into an hypothesis and retains throughout the sceptical temper which is its basis." For the ancient ideal of a body of demonstrated knowledge, Macmurray claimed that science had substituted "the deliberate development through experimental criticism of a continuous body of theory, the unending effort to substitute for the mere fact of belief the deliberate acceptance of belief upon rational grounds." Although the theory of knowledge which Macmurray eventually developed[8] bears a superficial resemblance to much in Dewey, he was not in fact influenced directly by Dewey's writings. (The phrase "the quest *of* certainty," later made famous in the title of Dewey's Gifford Lectures as "the quest *for* certainty," occurs in Macmurray's paper.) While Macmurray became more and more convinced of the importance of action as a fundamental philosophical concept, it would not have been possible for him to rest in any form of pragmatic philosophy. His reflection on the nature of scientific activity may have led him to stress the importance of action, but his concern for religion, supported by his reading of the history of western thought, ensured that the quest for the personal would remain Macmurray's engrossing task.

RELIGION AND SCIENCE

Of the half-dozen essays which he published between 1925 and 1929, three show how his interest in science interacted with his interest in religion. In "Christianity — Pagan or Scientific"[9] he criticised orthodox Christianity for its devotion to the ideals of certainty and security which carries with it the emphasis on dogma characteristic of the life of the church. Urging that Christianity become scientific, Macmurray described scientific Christianity as "a Christianity which lives experimentally, holding all its doctrines as liable to modification or even rejection, accepting all its rules of organisation and its laws of conduct, as simply so much result of human experience to be used as working hypotheses and experimented with incessantly for their own development and reshaping." It is not inconceivable that if the churches had been able to act on this advice, they would be in a stronger position to deal with their problems today.

Macmurray's admiration for the scientific attitude is again manifest in "Beyond Knowledge"[10] where he discussed various conceptions of faith. He rejected any view in which faith is opposed to reason or is identified with either intuition or any element in mystical experience. Pointing out that the attitude adopted by science is the attitude of faith,[11] an attitude of will, a way of acting in the face of ignorance, he pointed out that in the New Testament the term faith is most frequently contrasted not with knowledge but with fear, the attitude of mind which makes practical achievement of any kind impossible. When Jesus charged his disciples with being afraid and having little faith, he did not mean that they failed to subscribe to a set of religious beliefs but that they lacked confidence. Claiming that "fear masquerading as the need for security is still in the main our master," he later defined faith as "that attitude of consciousness which is completely triumphant over fear." Macmurray's conception of faith is ultimately rooted in his battle experience and combines the results of his reflection on scientific activity with what he learned from undertaking a critical rereading, with the trained eye of a classical scholar, of the Christian gospels and writings of Paul.

In "Objectivity in Religion"[12] Macmurray set the stage for all his subsequent thinking about religion, the human activity which remained his major philosophical preoccupation. Beginning with the assertion that "the whole of religion is rooted in the idea of God" he rejected all the traditional proofs of the existence of God, first on the general Kantian ground that existence is not a predicate and cannot be proved, and secondly on the ground that it is more important to discuss how we are to conceive the nature of the reality which we call God. Seeking an adequate statement of the problem, he asked, "Is the supreme reality of the world properly described as God or as matter or as life, or in some other way?" The significance of the three alternatives (much discussed in the twenties) becomes clearer in his further assertion that to say that God exists "means that the ultimate reality of the universe is such that it can satisfy religious demands. God is therefore necessarily personal. . . . there can be no question of an impersonal God. The phrase is a contradiction in terms." One may well doubt whether this statement could be justified, but it indicates how Macmurray's mind was working. In the history of Christian theology there have been disputes about whether it is appropriate to speak of "personality *in* God," the older trinitarian conception, or of "the personality *of* God," the more recent mode. The major difference between the Greek and the Christian conception of God lies in the fact that whereas the Greeks certainly appeared to think of God in an impersonal manner, Christian teaching (in so far as it is founded on the reported teachings of Christ) represented God as having the highly personal characteristic of love. The difference is vividly illustrated by comparing Aristotle's famous words "God moves the world as one who is loved . . ." with the even more famous Christian text "God so loved the world . . . ." If God is to be thought of as loving His creation, then indeed He must be conceived in personal terms, and Macmurray, thinking primarily of Christianity, asserted that "the relations which are the stuff of religious life are personal relations," a view which was to become fundamental in his philosophy. This remark is in striking contrast with A. N. Whitehead's often quoted statement that "religion is what a man does with his solitariness," a statement which must be almost totally incomprehensible to anyone familiar with the teaching of the founder of Christianity. Macmurray frequently warned against the confusion of religion with mysticism, a form in which religion *may* manifest itself but which cannot be identified as its essence. Whitehead's remark[13] is certainly more reminiscent of Plotinus, the fountainhead of western mysticism, with his "flight of the alone to the alone" than of anything in the teaching of Christ who asserted unequivocally that the two great commandments are to love God and one's neighbour. Neighbours are easy to love in theory when one is alone, but the Christian view is that they are to be loved in all their unlovableness by administering to their personal and practical needs.

THE FORM OF THE PERSONAL

Looking at the history of philosophy since the Renaissance, Macmurray saw the dominant problem as that of the nature of the self — not of God or the world or society.[14] He detected two main periods in modern philosophy corresponding roughly with the rise of the physical and the biological sciences. In the first, running from the time of Descartes to the French revolution, the self was conceived mathematically as an undifferentiated unit or substance,[15] while in the second, running up to the first world war, the self was conceived organically. Neither the mathematical nor the organic mode of conceiving the self is adequate to the nature of the personal, and Macmurray concluded that the major problem set to philosophy in the twentieth century, which has seen the blossoming of the psychological sciences, is that of working out the category or "form" of the personal. In the decade from 1928 to 1938 Macmurray in several books and articles stated the problem in various ways but could find no satisfactory solution. The problem seemed to him urgent both theoretically and practically. Without any clear conception of the nature of the personal, the psychological sciences were liable to develop an inadequate or even distorted account of human nature, while politically and socially any planning was likely to proceed on the assumption that the state and society were essentially organic in nature. If the field of personal relations is that of religion, then religion too, in the absence of any clear concept of the personal, must decline and its place be taken by the organic impersonal state. Holding that only through involvement in the mutuality of personal relations does a self reach full maturity as a person, Macmurray feared that the detached impersonal attitude of the scientific observer might indeed gain important objective knowledge about human behaviour but would fail to reach the level of personal knowledge best exemplified in the personal relation known as friendship. Not until the Gifford Lectures of 1953 was Macmurray able to offer an analysis of the category of the personal and to distinguish clearly between the theory of the personal as properly a subject for philosophical investigation and the objective behavioural knowledge of man in the abstract obtained by psychological and scientific methods.

Macmurray's constant preoccupation with the need to reach a satisfactory account of religion in general and Christianity in particular early led him to two important conclusions. First, he became convinced that the attempt on the part of theologians to work out Christian theology in the thought forms and language moulds which had been cast by the Greek mind with its characteristically aesthetic apperception of the world had had a fundamentally distorting effect on Christian thought. Secondly, like many other students of Christianity, he had been puzzled by the way in which a Christian culture, professedly based on the centrality in human life of the emotion of love, could accept and attempt to live by the Stoic philosophy which regards all emotion as a disturbing element to be eradicated as far as possible. Aware of this anomaly, Edwin Hatch, the ecclesiastical historian,[16] had suggested that the main task facing the Christian church was that of learning to adopt Christian theory before attempting to convert the world to Christian practice.

CHRISTIANITY AND COMMUNISM

Macmurray had just launched his first attack on Stoicism when an event occurred which was to have a major influence on his development. Sometime in 1930 he was asked to partake in a conference of distinguished literary men, theologians, and philosophers organised by J.H. Oldham. The question set for discussion was of frightening simplicity: what is Christianity? After protracted discussion the group reported that they were unable to reach an answer and said that they could not be expected to do so until they first studied two other problems, the place of sex in human life and the nature of communism. At this time communism was frequently described as a new kind of religion and taken to be the major rival of Christianity in the western world. In his *Creative Society* (sub-titled, *A Study in the Relation of Christianity to Communism*), Macmurray describes the plight of the Christian who does not know what his religion is nor what it stands for and yet is expected to act in terms of it over against his rival the communist, who is equipped with virtually infallible authorities and a precise philosophical doctrine. While not neglecting the problem of sex, which he tackled in the essay entitled "The Virtue of Chastity,"[17] Macmurray chose to throw himself for some years into the serious study of Marx and Marxism. This resulted in a spate of books and articles in which he either expounded the communist position for the benefit of the British public which he judged to be insularly and dangerously ignorant, or criticised elements in communist thought from the standpoint of one firmly convinced that Christianity properly understood and interpreted was the sounder doctrine.

Macmurray's interest in Marxism in the early thirties reflects the prevalent mood of British intellectuals contemplating the rapid growth of fascism and the total futility of the ruling conservative government. Hoping as he did to find that some synthesis of elements in Marxism and Christian doctrine might be possible, Macmurray is open to the criticism that his interpretation of Marx is coloured by overemphasising the points of agreement in communist and Christian social theory.[18] The Marxist doctrine of the unity of theory and practice was bound to have special appeal to one already inclined to give action priority over mere thought. At this time too, Macmurray professed an adherence to materialism which, though intelligible as a reaction against the otherworldliness which he disliked in Greek philosophy, does not appear to be wholly consistent with elements in his personalist philosophy. His natural sympathy with the Marxist criticism of Hegelian idealism was no doubt a powerful factor leading to his strongly expressed antagonism to the idealist element in much contemporary religious thought.[19] In two vitally important respects, however, Macmurray found himself seriously at odds with Marxism: in the first place he regarded the Marxist interpretation of religion as fundamentally misguided, and secondly he criticised dialectical materialism as seriously deficient philosophically in that it could rise no higher than an organic interpretation of the world, and has no place for truly human or personal activity.

NEW REFINEMENTS

From Macmurray's period of wrestling with the relations between Christianity and communism (roughly 1930-35) there emerged important consequences both for his religious thought and for the development of his philosophical position. First, having criticised institutional Christianity for its adherence to Greek modes of thought, Macmurray undertook the difficult task of re-interpreting the nature of Christianity. This he carried through in *The Clue to History* (not published until 1938 but actually completed several years earlier) which, while one of his more difficult books (for he had to cut through layers of misunderstanding accumulated over centuries) is of central importance to an understanding of Macmurray as a religious philosopher. Whereas Whitehead[20] had inserted what he called "the supreme moment in religious history," that is, "the life of Christ as a revelation of the nature of God and His agency," between Plato's conviction that the divine element in the world is a persuasive and not a coercive agency and the Platonic formulation of Christian theology in Alexandria and Antioch, Macmurray insists that Jesus was in no sense a philosopher of the Greek type but belonged to the great tradition of Hebrew prophets who had always thought of "history as the act of God." Characterising the Hebraic consciousness as essentially religious, communal and practical, he distinguishes it sharply both from the Greek which is theoretical and aesthetic and from the Roman which is technical and pragmatic. This triadic classification of modes of consciousness reappears in philosophical form in the Gifford Lectures as a distinction between the types of apperception which underlie different modes of morality. His interpretation of the Hebraic consciousness as practical and anti-dualist also led Macmurray to further insights into the nature of action and intention.

Secondly, Macmurray's perception of the metaphysical inadequacy of the Cartesian dualism of mind and matter was greatly sharpened. In "The Dualism of Mind and Matter"[21] he referred to Lovejoy's conclusion that the dualism is inevitable and revolt pointless but argued that there is no need for a new philosophical construction to assume that dualism as its starting point. What might be described as the Stoic dualism between reason and feeling also came under attack. Macmurray refused to admit that human rationality consisted simply in the capacity to reason or make inferences, but argued that rationality is essentially a capacity for objectivity and therefore could be identified as a characteristic of both thought and feeling.[22] Perhaps the most important stepping stone towards his definitive position was his 1938 paper, "What is Action?"[23] Ludicrously misunderstood by his fellow symposiasts, Macmurray was in fact attacking the basic Cartesian presuppositions of modern philosophy. The full scope of his attack, however, was not yet clear, and it was his rereading in the early forties of Kant's *Critique of Practical Reason* with its doctrine of the primacy of practical reason that enabled him to give his main argument the form which it has in the Gifford Lectures.

THE GIFFORD LECTURES

It has been said that every man's end is in his beginning. This is certainly true of Macmurray. All the major themes developed in the Gifford Lectures are to be found in embryo form in his early writings. In this paper I have endeavoured merely to sketch some of the incidents and experiences and deeprooted convictions which lie behind the complex metaphysical argument of the Gifford Lectures. It is perhaps not too much to say that the dominating philosophical problem for Macmurray has always been how to make sense of the claim, central to the religion in which he was brought up, that the divine element in the universe is personal. Writers must always make difficult choices about how and in what order they will present what they have to say, and these choices may sometimes mislead the unwary reader. The first volume of the Gifford Lectures, *The Self as Agent,* with its almost uncompromising insistence on the primacy of action may leave the impression that Macmurray is some kind of belated pragmatist. Nothing could be wider of the truth. Throughout his whole career Macmurray's chief concern had been the human condition. His major thesis, to which all else leads up, is that "the personal relation of persons is constitutive of personal existence" or in even simpler terms that " 'I' exist only as one element in the complex 'You and I'." It is only in the second volume, *Persons in Relation,* that Macmurray attempts to show how the mutuality of persons implies the primacy of action. It might be said that by breaking away from the metaphysical solitariness of the thinking self over against the world as object and by adopting the standpoint of the self as agent existing in dynamic relation with the world, Macmurray has made it possible for philosophers to take seriously the insight of the poet — "no man is an island entire of himself; every man is a piece of the continent, a part of the main." Perhaps the time for paying lip service to this truth is past and philosophical action is needed.

Footnotes

[1] Just as very different answers would be given to the two questions: what is physics? and what is physics about?

[2] *Freedom in the Modern World* (London, 1932), p. 68.

[3] "Concerning the History of Philosophy," *Proceedings of the Aristotelian Society, Supp.* 25 (1951): 23, 11.

[4] *Search for Reality in Religion,* the Swarthmore Lecture of 1965 (London: 1965, 1969), pp. 17–18. This pamphlet contains a brief autobiography. Its title is virtually descriptive of Macmurray's philosophical career.

[5] Ibid., p. 21.

[6] For a detailed account of this episode see Roy Harrod's biography of Lindemann, *The Prof* (London: 1959), pp. 17–27.

[7] See "The Function of Experiment in Knowledge," *Proceedings of the Aristotelian Society* 27 (1926–27): 193–212, from which the following quotations are taken.

[8] Expounded mainly in *Interpreting the Universe* (London: 1933), which should be read along with the Gifford Lectures. It is worth noting that Macmurray, who had heard M. Schlick lecturing in London in the late twenties, fully accepted the need for verification in philosophy (see chap. 3, "Interpretation and Verification"). Whereas the logical positivists demanded verification in sense perception, Macmurray suggested that verification might be sought in action.

[9] *Hibbert Journal* 24 (1926): 421–33.

[10] In *Adventure: The Faith of Science and the Science of Faith,* ed. B. Streeter (London: 1927).

[11] A. N. Whitehead in *Science and the Modern World* (New York, 1925) talks of the faith of the scientist.

[12] Included in *Adventure.*

[13] Whitehead's *Religion in the Making* (New York, 1926) and Macmurray's *The Structure of Religious Experience* (London, 1936) reveal two widely contrasting conceptions of religion, one from the organic, the other from the personalist point of view.

[14] See "The Unity of Modern Problems," *Journal of Philosophical Studies* 4 (1929), 162–79. Macmurray's general thesis about the centrality of the problem of the self is well illustrated in John Laird's *Problems of the Self* (London, 1917).

[15] Each period of course revealed considerable internal diversity. The scepticism of Hume, for example, represented the dissolution of the substance conception of the self.

[16] *The Influence of Greek Ideas on Christianity,* the Hibbert Lectures of 1888 (New York, 1957). Macmurray had not in fact read this book, but it substantiates Macmurray's thesis about the distorting effect of Greek philosophy in Christian teaching.

[17] See *Reason and Emotion* (London, 1935, 1962), pp. 116–144.

[18] See, for example, Elizabeth Lam, "Does Macmurray Understand Marx?" *The Journal of Religion* 20 (1940): 47–65.

[19] See *Idealism Against Religion* (London, 1944).

[20] See *Adventures of Ideas* (New York, 1933).

[21] *Philosophy* 10 (1935): 264–78.

[22] See "The Nature of Reason," *Proceedings of the Aristotelian Society* 35 (1936): 137–48, and *Interpreting the Universe,* chap. 6.

[23] *Proceedings of the Aristotelian Society, Supp.* 17 (1938): 69–85.

The Rational Theology of Thomas Hobbes/

W. H. F. BARNES

Hobbes' views on theology and his account of the Christian faith have been little studied because of the verdict passed upon them by most of his contemporaries. He was hostile to all scholasticism in theology and the theologians of his day repaid him by pinning the label "atheist" firmly upon him. But though he was an idiosyncratic Christian, there is no ground for supposing him an atheist. On the contrary: if rational theology is taken to mean the finding of reasons for believing that God exists and that He has certain attributes and for having any further beliefs about what we might call the Kingdom of God, i.e. any further facts· about the world and human nature which depend on the existence of God, then Hobbes' fundamental Biblical account of the Christian religion does not exclude but is actually supplemented by some rational theology.

Professor Howard Warrender says that "Hobbes seems to have held that reason leads us to a knowledge of the existence of God as first mover."[1] What does Hobbes say on this matter? He says that "by the light of nature it may be known that there is a God." (2:27,198n.)[2] We may reasonably ask: Granting that the light of nature is some sort of rational capacity for knowledge, how did Hobbes suppose it operated in this case? For there is no attempt in the *Elements of Law* or the *De Cive* to prove, or give a rational justification for belief in the existence of, God.[3] *Leviathan* takes the matter a stage further in Chapter XII, which is devoted to religion. At the end of his previous chapter, "Of the difference of manners" (i.e., morals), Hobbes had run into speaking of credulity to which men are disposed by ignorance of natural causes and by anxiety for the future, which leads a man to enquire into the causes of things. Hobbes is then led to speak of curiosity in the following terms: "Curiosity, or love of the knowledge of causes, draws a man from consideration of the effect, to seek the cause; and again, the cause of that cause; till of necessity he must come to this thought at last, that there is some cause, whereof there is no former cause, but is eternal: which is what men call God. So that it is impossible to make any profound enquiry into natural causes, without being inclined thereby to believe there is one God eternal; though they cannot have any idea of him in their minds, answerable to his nature." (3:92) He compares one who so proceeds to a blind man who, being warmed by fire, after he has heard men talking of warming themselves by fire, conceives of something as the cause of the heat he feels, though he can have no idea of it such as those who see it have. So a man may conceive of God as cause of "the visible things of this world and their admirable order" (3:92), yet have no idea of that cause. Further, those who do not enquire into natural causes feign from ignorance invisible powers to do them good or harm. Though fear is the natural seed[4] of superstition, acknowledging one God "may more easily be derived" from enquiring into natural causes by which a man "should at last come to this, that there must be . . . one First Mover; . . . that is, a first, and an eternal cause of all things . . . ." (3:96) It is, then, disinterested curiosity which gives rise to belief in one God; fear, which hinders the search into the causes of other things, makes men feign Gods. The language Hobbes uses—a man "must at last come to this thought," "shall at last come to this"—strongly suggests that, on his view, belief in the existence of God is, for the man who enquires into causes, rational, and in some sense necessary.

In *De Corpore,* published a few years after *Leviathan,* Hobbes speaks rather differently. The man, he says, who sets out to trace cause and effect will "not be able to proceed eternally, but wearied will at last give over, without knowing whether it were possible for him to proceed to an end or not. But whether we suppose the world to be finite or infinite, no absurdity will follow. . . . I cannot therefore commend those that boast that they have demonstrated, by reasons drawn from natural things, that the world had a beginning." (1: 412-13) At first consideration, this may seem to be at variance with what Hobbes says in *Leviathan*. But there is no contradiction. What he says here is that one cannot demonstrate, i.e. prove, that there is a first event; what he says in *Leviathan* is that one concludes that there must be an eternal cause. To maintain that God is the eternal cause of the series of events in time is consistent with holding either that the series of events in time is finite or that it is infinite.[5]

The *Leviathan* passage contains also a brief statement of the Argument from Design, viz., that from the "admirable order" of visible things "a man may *conceive* there is a cause of them." Though not stated as a proof, this appears to be an argument of some sort. In two other passages Hobbes adumbrates a similar argument. In one he says that it is "very hard to believe" that sex differences and the organs of sense and memory could be "the work of anything that had not understanding" (7:126) ; in the other he says that those who cannot see that generation and nutrition have been "constructed by some mind" must themselves be "without a mind." (LW 2:6)

These passages make it abundantly clear that Hobbes was — to put the matter minimally — not merely not disposed to reject belief in God, but that he thought there was good reason for that belief.[6] I put the matter in this way because, as will appear, there is need to draw distinctions. Mr. K.C. Brown, who collected and considered the passages to which I have referred,[7] draws the conclusion that Hobbes rejected the First Mover argument for God, but accepted the Argument from Design. He is led to take this line in order to reconcile seeming discrepancies which he finds in Hobbes. He quotes from the work "Considerations upon the Reputation, Loyalty, Manners and Religion of Thomas Hobbes," in which Hobbes, at the age of seventy-four, writes of himself:

> For a third argument of atheism, you [Wallis] put that he [Hobbes] says: "besides the creation of the world, there is no argument to prove a Deity"; and "that it cannot be evinced by any argument that the world had a beginning"; and that "whether it had or no is to be decided not by argument but by the magistrate's authority." (4:427)

In reply Hobbes, after making the point that whether the world has a beginning or not is, on his view, to be *decided* by Scripture and the chief magistrate's part is to interpret the Scripture,[8] goes on:

> As for arguments from natural reason, neither you nor any other, have hitherto brought nay, except the creation, that has not made it more doubtful to many than it was before.

Mr. Brown takes the argument from creation to refer here to the argument from design because he regards Hobbes' rejection of the argument that the world had a beginning as a rejection of the First Cause argument. It seems to me much more likely that the argument from creation (which Hobbes accepts here) is the argument that the world, *whether it is finite or infinite in time,* i.e., whether there is or is not any event which was the initiating cause of all subsequent events, must have as a series of events in time an eternal cause. The argument he rejected in *De Corpore* is the argument that the world had a *beginning,* i.e., a temporally first event. Whether it had, or had not, is a matter of Christian doctrine, to be decided on the basis of interpreted scripture. The fact that it has a cause, God, outside the temporal sequence and therefore eternal, is discovered by "natural reason."

If it is accepted that the argument from creation is the argument that there must be a First Cause, then, since Hobbes in the passage from "Considerations, etc." is implicitly rejecting all other arguments for God, he is rejecting the argument from design. There might seem to be reason for thinking he did not accept any such argument, in his statement elsewhere: "That which we call design, which is reasoning and thought after thought, cannot be properly attributed to God." (5:14) To speak of design would be to imply not merely that God exists and is the eternal cause of the world, but to claim knowledge of how he operated to bring it about. But, in fact, Hobbes' reference in *Leviathan* is to "the visible things of this world, and their admirable order" in which "a man may conceive there is a cause of them." (3:93) I take Hobbes to be saying simply that both the existence and the order of the world require a First Cause, and not to be concerned to argue that, even if *a* world could come into existence without a First Cause, *this* admirably ordered world could not.

The question we must now ask is: What, on Hobbes' view, are we rationally justified in saying about God, once we are convinced of His existence? There are two not easily reconcilable strands in Hobbes' thought. First, in the earlier works, *The Elements of Law* and *De Cive*, our subjection to the Law of God is accepted. The questions canvassed are: How is this to be reconciled with our subjection to a human sovereign? (4:170-71; 2:289-91) And, in *De Cive*, what worship of God does natural reason assign to us? (2:213-16) The answer which Hobbes gives to this second question (which alone concerns us here) is later repeated in more forthright terms in *Leviathan:*

> . . . it is a part of rational worship, to speak considerately of God; for it argues a fear of him, and fear, is a confession of his power. Hence followeth, that the name of God is not to be used rashly, and to no purpose unless it be by way of oath, and by order of the common-wealth, to make judgements certain; or between common-wealths, to avoid war. And that disputing God's nature is contrary to his honour: for it is supposed, that in this natural kingdom of God, there is no other way to know any thing, but by natural reason; that is, from the principles of natural science; which are so far from teaching us any thing of God's nature, as they cannot teach us our own nature, nor the nature of the smallest creature living. And therefore, when men out of the principles of natural reason, dispute of the attributes of God, they but dishonour him: for in the attributes which we give to God, we are not to consider the signification of philosophical truth; but the signification of pious intention, to do him the greatest honour we are able. (3:353-54; cf. 2:217)

Yet when Hobbes himself became engaged in argument about God, he was led to say quite a number of things about Him which do not fit with the doctrine that all we can truly say of Him is that He exists. In various places God is described by Hobbes as corporeal substance (4:383), as "an infinitely fine spirit" (4:310) — spirit being "thin, fluid, transparent, invisible body (4:309) — as "somewhere" (4:393), as a *spirit corporeal* and *infinitely pure* (4:384, 336). Much of what he has to say in this vein clearly arises from his contention that "incorporeal spirit" is a self-contradictory term, since only bodies exist, and spirit must be a body. In another passage Hobbes, after referring to the existency, infiniteness, incomprehensibility, unity and ubiquity of God, says:

> First, all men by nature had an opinion of God's existency; but of his other attributes not so soon, but by reasoning and by degrees. And for the attributes of the true God, they were never suggested but by the Word of God written. (4:293)

It seems that natural reason, as well as producing the conviction of God's existence, in the case of the Christian also tells us what attributes we can assign to God. It does this on the basis of what is suggested to us by Scripture, though the formulation of these suggestions by reason takes time. There is a problem in that some of the things Hobbes says about God, e.g., God is corporeal, seem to express "a philosophical truth," and not to be honorific; and they do not fit comfortably into Hobbes' general picture.

If we exclude these for the moment, there remain two quite distinct elements in our cognitive relation to God. We can reach the truth of God's existence by reason without the aid of Scripture. The attributes we assign to God, however, are based on suggestions taken from Scripture and are honorific. We significantly praise his goodness, magnify his power and bless his felicity. To do so is neither contrary to, nor lacking in, reason. For it is a dictate of natural reason, and a law of God, to speak in this way of Him. (3:348) To do so is rational as morality is rational; it is acting in accordance with the laws which God has, by means of reason and the Scriptures, laid down for men in their own interest.

The sophisticated union of rationalism and scripturalism in this doctrine has gone unnoticed because it has not been appreciated that for Hobbes "natural reason" operates theoretically in scientific thinking and practically in morals and religion. While in *De Cive* he spoke quite consistently of "what manner of worship of God natural reason doth assign us" (2:213), later, in the passage quoted from *Leviathan* he says that we cannot *know* anything except by natural reason (and cannot, therefore, know God's nature), but he is able to speak of *"rational* worship" because natural reason in its practical aspect dictates the form of that worship.

What we say in the Christian liturgy is rationally justified, not as knowledge but as an act of worship performed in obedience to God. Hobbes, when he refers to speaking of God in such a way as to honour him, does not think it enough merely to use any words with the intention of honouring God. There are properly honorific forms of expression. To use only such expressions in worship is the dictate of natural reason. To dispute about God's attributes is to misuse natural reason by seeking to apply it theoretically in a field where it has no validity. How we are to come by the proper expressions of worship he does not make very clear. He suggests on one occasion that we are to choose them in the light of answers to two questions: How are we inclined to think, and accordingly to speak, of God? And is it fitting so to speak of Him? In "Considerations, etc." he says that "it is by all Christians confessed, that God is *incomprehensible*," and continues:

> What then ought we to say of him? What attributes are to be given him *(not speaking otherwise than we think, nor otherwise than is fit,)* by those who mean to honour him? None but such as Mr. Hobbes has set down, namely, expressions of reverence, such as are in use amongst men for signs of honour and not such as neither reason nor scripture hath approved for honourable. This is the doctrine that Mr. Hobbes hath written; both in his *Leviathan,* and in his *De Cive,* and when occasion serves, maintains. What kind of attribute, I pray you, is *immaterial,* or *incorporeal* substance? Where do you find it in the Scripture? (4:426)

We can now return to the status of the assertion that God is corporeal, and other assertions about Him that appear to claim truth. It may be that Hobbes regarded the assertion that God is corporeal as, in part, simply rejecting the absurdity of saying that he is incorporeal and so far as it asserted anything, saying simply that He is something, i.e. that He exists. In general, those non-honorific assertions about God he makes from time to time are to be regarded as analysing what is meant by saying God exists.

Hobbes' fundamental tenet in natural theology is that the world must have an eternal cause and it is this which we call God. Though this was a traditional doctrine it fitted perfectly into Hobbes' philosophy. (In the Short Tract[9] he had recognised two kinds of causal agents, that which moves by its inherent power and that which moves by motion received from another. But he soon came to exclude the former kind of agency from the world of motion. It returns, however, in the conception of God as a corporeal being with inherent and, as cause of the world, absolute power. It is perhaps not surprising that some readers of Hobbes should suppose that if God is corporeal, He is either the world or part of the world. But Hobbes says nothing to justify such an inference and goes out of his way to criticise those who hold that the world is God. "For by the word God we understand the world's cause; but in saying that the world is God, they say that it hath no cause, that is as much, as there is no God." (2:213-14)

There is a reference in Aubrey which might seem to suggest that only timidity prevented Hobbes from embracing a Spinozistic pantheism:

> When Spinoza's *Tractatus Theologico-Politicus* first came out, Mr. Edmund Waller sent it to my lord of Devonshire and desired him to send him word what Mr. Hobbes said of it.
> He told me he had cut thorough him a barre's length, for he durst not write so boldly.[10]

The purport of the passage, however, is not at all clear. It attributes to Hobbes the statement that he (Hobbes) did not dare to go as far as Spinoza. But in what respect, we are not told. Could Hobbes have had in mind Spinoza's complete divorce of natural right from reason? or his notion that a contract has no binding force but Utility?[11] In both these ways Spinoza went farther than Hobbes. Or could it be in respect of Spinoza's pantheism? There is a passage in Hobbes which does at first suggest a leaning towards pantheism. He is discussing the concepts of substance, essence and body. Speaking of body he distinguishes body that is pure and simple, i.e., body of one and the same kind, from a mixture of bodies in which the parts of the bodies mix while retaining their simplicity. Two waters, one of the river, the other a mineral water, may look the same, yet when put together be visually indistinguishable from milk. It must be that the parts remain separate, since two bodies cannot be in the same place. How, he asks, has the mineral water changed the appearance of the whole water "and yet not being every where, and in every part of the water?" As it has done so, Hobbes asks whether we can doubt that God who is a spirit (that is, a thin, fluid invisible body) "can make and change all species and kinds of body as he pleaseth." (4:309-10)

The doctrine that God is a body operating amongst the bodies that make up the world, entails that God is a different substance from the world, though spatially intermingled with it.[12] It excludes, therefore, the doctrine that the world *is* God. As well as the uncertainty as to which doctrine in Spinoza Hobbes was referring in the remark reported by Aubrey, there is a further caution that needs to be exercised in interpreting the remark. On may admire the boldness of another in going further along a line of thought than one would oneself have dared to go, even though one would not have wished or thought it reasonable to go so far. We need not therefore suppose that Hobbes embraced any doctrine, pantheistic, atheistic or non-Christian, which he was not prepared to disclose. He remained within the Church of England, accepting during an illness, the offer of Dr. Cosins, the Bishop of Durham, to pray for him and to administer the Sacrament. (LW 1:xvi) Later (LW 4:303), when attacked on the subject of his Christianity, he proposed that the sincerity if his faith be referred to Bishop Cosins.

His doctrinal position is that little beyond the existence of God can be established by reason. All that the Christian has to believe for salvation is contained in the assertion that Jesus is the Messiah. (4:174) In this doctrine and elsewhere in the Scriptures there is much that defies comprehension. But we are neither to use what is said to overthrow what experience and reason teach us, nor to engage in profitless dispute about its meaning; but to believe it for our profit and betterment. "For it is with the mysteries of our religion, as with wholesome pills for the sick, which swallowed whole, have the virtue to cure; but chewed, are for the most part cast up again without effect."[13]

Footnotes

[1] Howard Warrender, "The Place of God in Hobbes' Philosophy," *Political Studies* 8 (1960): 52.

[2] References in parentheses are to the volume and page numbers of *The English Works of Thomas Hobbes*, ed. Sir William Molesworth, 11 vols. (London, 1839–1845) or, where the numbers are preceded by "LW," to the Latin works, *Hobbes' Opera Latina*, ed. Molesworth, 5 vols. (London, 1839–45).

[3] *De Cive* XV.14.

[4] In Hobbes' own words, "the natural seed of that, which every one in himself calleth religion; and in them that worship, or fear that power otherwise than they do, is superstition." (3:93) This could be interpreted as, by implication, asserting that all religion is superstition. But there is no compelling reason so to interpret it. It is a *fact* that people call those who worship other deities or the same deity in different ways than they do, superstitious. And in the next chapter Hobbes says explicitly that, while perhaps the Gods of the Gentiles are the creations of fear, the one God "may more easily be derived from the desire men have to know the causes of natural bodies . . . ." (3:95)

[5] In thinking thus Hobbes was not drawing any distinction between First Cause and First Mover, since all events for him consist entirely of movements.

[6] The statement that "Hobbes maintained that Scripture, and not reason, is our only warrant for believing in God's existence," cannot be defended. S. I. Mintz, *The Hunting of Leviathian* (Cambridge, 1962), p. 43.

[7] In his "Hobbes' Grounds for Belief in a Deity," *Philosophy* 37 (1962): 336–344.

[8] Not a negligible correction.

[9] *The Elements of Law*, ed. F. Thonnies (Cambridge, 1928), pp. 193–201. This manuscript treatise, first attributed to Hobbes and published by Tonnies in 1889, is almost certainly Hobbes' first written work on philosophy.

[10] John Aubrey, *Brief Lives*, ed. A. Powell (London, 1949), p. 255.

[11] This former view finds explicit expression in Spinoza's *Tractatus-Politicus*, II.5, but it is already implicit in *Tractatus Theologico-Politicus* V, XVI, which chapter also contains the latter. *Spinoza, The Political Works*, ed. A. G. Wernham. (Oxford, 1958), pp. 93, 127, 131.

[12] The whole of this passage shows the influence of Stoic doctrines: (i) God is the purest body; (ii) God pervades all things. H.F.A. Von Arnim, *Stoicorum Veterum Fragmenta*, 2 (Stuttgart, 1968), no. 1029. This doctrine is an application of the more general Stoic doctrine of the mixture of one body with another, in which one totally permeates the other. Ibid., 2, part I, cap. I, art 11.

[13] (3 360) It is consistent with this acceptance of mystery that Hobbes should regard "cheerful, charitable and upright behaviour towards men" as "better signs of religion than the zealous maintaining of controverted doctrines." (4:433)

The Elusive Self and Practice/

H. D. LEWIS

The problem of personal identity has always been a central one for philosophy, and it has also obvious ramifications, of a very wide-ranging nature, for all practical and social problems. It is not likely that we shall have any profound understanding of practical issues, in personal ethics or in politics, unless we have a sound appreciation of what individual persons are like, how they feel and react and how, if I may use a somewhat old-fashioned term, their ultimate destiny is to be conceived. We may have moved very far from the days when eminent thinkers wrote elaborate works with titles like Bosanquet's *The Value and Destiny of the Individual,* and there are those, like myself, who believe that something has been lost as well as gained in the process. But even the most avant-garde and fashionable of down to earth contemporary philosophers find their thoughts centred as much as ever on the question of personal identity, and they seem to find this no less inescapable in dealing with legal and ethical problems than in the remoter spheres of epistemology and speculative thought. Accordingly, an attempt to indicate (though for obvious reasons in outline only) the relevance of the views I have defended elsewhere to our practical concerns and attitudes may be a not inappropriate way of paying tribute to the work of one like John Macmurray, whose thought never strayed very far from the sphere of practice.

THE SELF AND VALUE

The view which I have been defending in my other writings, is that every person has an inner or non-observable awareness of his own experiences in having them and of himself as the unique begin who has these experiences though the experiences themselves could have been different; and in memory, I have maintained, we are firmly aware of a continuous identity of which we have further less direct indication in appropriate evidence. The self, so conceived, is elusive in the sense that it cannot be described in the finality of its distinctness. But there is nothing mysterious about it in any other way. It is not known a priori or as a postulate—or pushed in some way out of the picture. Everyone knows himself as being himself, whether he reflects upon this or not. This does not give us an indestructible soul, such as Plato and in our own day McTaggart thought we had. Nothing finite is indestructible. But we have an awareness in ourselves and in our own lives of our own existence as non-material beings, having an ultimate irreducible identity and capable, as we have already existed for some time, of continuing to exist—perhaps in vastly different conditions. What importance has this for our further understanding of ourselves and the cultural and social setting in which our main problems and practical expectations appear?

In answer let me note firstly that, if we hold the view that the self, in its most essential nature, is other than the body and also more than its passing states, however much involved in the latter, then we have an entity which can be conceived as existing after the dissolution of our bodies and the end of our present existence. What form this could take is another matter. There is a case for saying that some sort of body is needed to be a focus for activity and experience, and for identification by others than ourselves. But this could be a very different body, and there is no case for saying that it is through the body that we are particularized. The self, in itself, is the most distinctive particular there is. Some would also hold, as I do, that the idea of a totally disembodied existence is not to be altogether dismissed. But whatever we say on these scores, we have, in the notion of the elusive self already set forth, an entity capable at least of existing under conditions very different from those to which we are subject now.

It does not follow that the self *will* survive. There is no inevitable immortality. To hold that we do survive we must have additional reasons, provided for some by psychical research, for others by metaphysics or religion. But the possibility cannot begin to be entertained if we are convinced of the soundness of the views about the nature of persons which hold most sway in philosophy at present. The death of the body on those views spells the death of all. That is not a reason for rejecting them. They must be considered on their merits as accounts of what we find consciousness and selfhood to be. But if the way is open to think of ourselves as having a further existence, and if we have further reason for supposing that we have some destiny beyond our life as we know it now, then this could bring an additional perspective, perhaps of immense importance, in which to view the problems which confront us now. I hold, in fact, that our attitudes would be transformed, and that we could approach many problems with greater serenity and a more balanced judgment, if we were enabled to renew the sense of a deeper spirituality and hope which the thought of an existence not subject to our present limitations could bring.

I turn now to a point that has more obviously to do with practice, namely the bearing of my theme on the sense in which it may be said that value is personal. I have maintained that we cannot describe what each person is in his own essential being as known to himself, but it would be altogether wrong to regard the self so conceived as an appendage, a functionless further thing we carry around with us. Our experiences and dispositions could have been different, but they do *belong* to us in a peculiarly intimate, indissoluble way. I am in my experiences, even if I am more than them. My dispositions are also essentially *my* dispositions. They are not something of which I have charge or some particular stewardship, they are me; and to draw too rigid a wedge between the self, in its finality, and the course of all that happens to it could well be an even greater mistake than to reduce the self wholly to its passing states. However hard it may be to provide a satisfactory philosophical account of the relation of the self to the course of experience, and I doubt whether there is any more baffling philosophical problem than that (as may already be evident), the self is really in its experiences in the most intimate way. I need not have a pain at the moment, but if I do *I* feel it; it is I who think certain things, feel despondent or elated, like or dislike people, etc. I am not a thing apart from all this.

It follows that the distinctions of worth we make at all levels are really ascribable to each as a whole person. A man is entitled to be proud of his attainments, they are pre-eminently his; it is he who should be sorry for his shortcomings, or ashamed if shame is in order—they are also essentially *his*. No one should be encouraged to be indifferent to what his life is like or what he becomes. On the contrary we have a duty to cultivate the best that is in us, as our lot or situation allows. We cannot do this without other people, there is very little that we ever attain entirely on our own; but each of us has, all the same, a peculiar involvement in what he himself becomes, and also a duty to mind it.

This is, in itself, a matter of non-moral values, although there is the important moral duty indicated of promoting, in ourselves as in others, every sort of worth we can. A word should perhaps be interpolated here about the distinction of moral and non-moral good which is of such radical importance for good sense in ethics. Among non-moral goods are health and physical well-being, physical skills (in athletics, for example), artistic and intellectual attainment, personal relationships and qualities of character, like affection or courage. Opposed to these are non-moral evils, like pain, stupidity, insensitivity and excessive concern for oneself. We cannot change these directly at will, we cannot instantly summon up appropriate feelings of sorrow or kindness or boldness, although these and their like may be cultivated (or discouraged) as the case requires. Our natural endowment, and all, of good or ill, that circumstances do to these are the lot we have—they are gifts of nature or fortune. But they are no less personal for that reason, and a due regard for the delicately inward character of personal attainments and the peculiar significance they have for each in being the attainments of the unique and distinctive being he is, as known to himself and recognised by others, brings a peculiar flavour and subtlety, and an element of great dignity as well, to personal relations and the respect for persons which has often been accorded so central a place in ethics.

There could, indeed, be a case for the notion of respect for persons even if this were thought of in some less absolute way as a unique combination of certain properties or mental states. But I leave with you the suggestion, which I cannot follow up further now, that the most subtle and impressive feature of our regard for persons, at the reflective and non-reflective level alike, is found in the way each person is involved, in the distinctness and finality of his own being, in all his experiences.

This is peculiarly marked in our more intimate relationships, friendly or hostile; and I have tried to bring this out in my book, *The Elusive Mind,* in my discussion of what I take to be truly important in the notion of an *I-Thou* relationship as presented by Martin Buber and his followers. The sense that we are really dealing with "the other" brings a very special quality or dimension to our more intimate dealings with one another—and it should never be absent.

For similar reasons we should be very wary of collectivist ways of thinking even of non-moral worth. We can indeed speak of national pride or other good or bad characteristics of groups of people. But this is metaphor and generalisation. There is no proper bearer of any worth other than the individual. The "soul of a people" is metaphor. There are only individual souls; and if I may be pardoned again for referring to my own work, I have been at pains often to expose the ills that ensue from passing from useful metaphorical idioms to a more strict or literal form of collectivist notions of human relations. Few matters seem to me to have more relevance than this to major world issues of today.

When we turn to properly moral worth, the importance of heeding the finality and uniqueness of the distinctness of persons, as indicated earlier, is even more evident. No man, as the famous quotation has it, is an island. But we come very near to it in moral choice. Our aptitudes and our likes and dislikes are set for us together with the external features of the situations within which a choice must be made. So are our moral convictions at the time, or the light according to which we are judged. But how we respond when our duties seem to be in courses of action not in accord with what we most wish at the time—this is where we have to make an absolute choice which is not itself determined by character or environment or anything else. Such a choice can only be made by a self which is more than its formed character at the time, and what can this be other than the self in the sense in which it can not be characterised or observed?

Few will doubt that the restoration of the sense of responsibility, blunted by much in contemporary thought and practice and not least in influential sociological theories, is a great need of our time. I will not enlarge on a theme so evident in recent and contemporary history.

ON PRACTICE

This brings me to metaphysical and religious considerations that have a close bearing on practice. Many deny the finality of the distinctness of persons and hold, in many forms of monism and mystical philosophies or religions that the individual is eventually merged in the Absolute or in some Supreme Universal Self or Universal Mind. Various disciplines are meant to further this end. But if I am right, however much we may hope to attain closer union with God, or whatever takes his place in our system of thought, there is no absorption of the individual in the being of another, whether man or God. A finite being could always be eliminated, but, however restricted and dependent, the core of his being remains, as long as he exists, intact—now or hereafter.

Since much of the philosophical arguments for the alleged mystical elimination of the distinctness of persons turns on the seemingly contentless character of the "pure self," as allegedly disclosed to the mystic in the more distinctive introvert forms of his experience, it is important to note well that the way in which the self in its true being as known to itself, is without specifiable criteria of its distinctiveness, requires at *the same time* that it be recognised as ultimate and irreducible.

This has specific relevance to the religious and kindred practices by which it is sometimes hoped to attain to certain spiritual states. It calls for an involvement in the lives of others even in the more profoundly personal forms of spiritual devotion. But it also relates more directly to social problems as affording an essential corrective to excessively other-worldly forms of religious or metaphysical commitment or to other views which reduce the significance of the rich and varied course of our lives in this world and tend towards apathy and uniformity as opposed to vigour and creativity.

On the face of it the great religions of the East, and especially Hinduism and Buddhism, seem to favour more the collectivist and monistic attitudes which I oppose. But there is also much in the literature and history of these religions which supports another view, and there have also been raised recently distinguished voices, like those of Aurobindo, to plead for a more dynamic form of their own religions with greater recognition of the worth and variety of life as lived here and now.

To what extent metaphysical and religious attitudes affect practice and social policies is perhaps a moot point, and Aurobindo may himself have exaggerated the influence of the more other-worldly features of Indian philosophers and religions. But the influence is there and requires direction. In the case of Buddhism and, I should maintain, in some features of Hinduism also, there has been much distortion and misunderstanding of their basic notions and attitudes. The reluctance of Buddhist thinking to recognise some specifiable entities over and above our passing states could be looked at afresh with profit in the light of a subtler understanding of what precisely is the elusiveness of the self. We may find here, as in many other matters where recent controversy has sharpened our understanding—in thought about God's transcendence, for instance—that the Puli Canon is more on our side than against it.

I offer this as a suggestion which could be followed up much more exhaustively today than has hitherto been the case, and must leave it, for the moment at least, to those more expert than I to ponder. It seems to me a much more profitable line of investigation than that which would cast aside or question a tremendous spiritual heritage just because it seems, on a reading which may in part be misleading, to be inimical to urgent practical needs. If the needs of the whole person are to be considered in a balanced way, then there may be a strong case for continuing, or restoring when lost, a great spiritual tradition which we can now examine afresh and which may have a great deal to do with the rounded ordering of our lives in the world—as individuals and as members of society.

A further aspect of contemporary problems which is bound to be much in our minds when we think of practical issues is the upsurge of violence and unreason in our time. There are many aspects of this that must fall outside the scope of this paper. But there is one that has very close relevance to our theme. I refer to the extensive but unhealthy and perplexing preoccupation with violence and other excesses of passionate excitation on their own account. Why should these have so much fascination and appeal independently even of any further end they may be thought to promote? Part of the answer lies in the mismanagement of that inwardness of experience and the distinctness of persons to which we are prone in several ways. We resent the limitation imposed upon us by our finite nature which precludes our breaking wholly into the inner sanctuary of the lives of others. We expect to know them as they know themselves—or as God knows. This we think we attain when we catch people without the usual disguises, when convention and habit fall away, as in extremes of terror or excitation. The expectation is ill-founded, for whatever is accomplished in this way, it still does not give us a wholly un-mediated glimpse of "the other" as he is for himself: it is a per-sistently self-defeating enterprise which can become inflamed to the level of daemonic and ruthless destructiveness. The remedy is to understand ourselves better, as we are well equipped to do today, and to see our state and its limitations in a corrected per-spective which will enable us to balance the awareness of our essential inwardness or privacy, and the respect it deserves, with the properly realistic view of our place in the world around us and the lives of others. The right sort of subjectivism prescribes its own correlative realism, and there is much that may be done here by philosophical thought, as well as by more explicit exhorta-tion or censure, to induce the appropriate frame of mind. The influence of philosophy in the context of the layman's thoughts and attitudes is often more extensive than we think and nowhere to my mind more so than in matters like the one instanced here.

Nor is it only in the broad setting of politics or of explicitly religious situations that this has significance. I suggest that it could be followed up with great advantage by students of psychology and social pathology, and it could well help to break the stalemate of continuing a fruitless round of variations on themes of repression and complexes to which the practitioner, like the theorist, often only clings in desperation in the absence of any better schema for his work. We need a new and better psychology, and the way to attain it could well come from a better understanding of the inescapable inwardness of personal existence.

I have referred incidentally from time to time to religion, and this is a subject which cannot, in my view, ever be very far from social and political issues, however much we may also need to be on our guard to preserve the proper autonomy of these and the disciplines concerned with them. A central theme of religion is (in Whitehead's famous phrase) "what a man does with his solitariness." It is remarkable how much this has become a major concern in literature and life today. Even Bertrand Russell, in no sense a pietistic person, made a great deal of what he himself called "a sombre solitude" and the oppressiveness and fear that breeds in it. To this, the ultimate answer, in my view, is found in religion. At the core of most religions is this problem of inwardness and solitude. For some the way of salvation lies in escape to a wholly transcendent existence where finitude and its problems no longer oppress us. For others there are ways in which the transcendent may come into the citadels of our finite being without total disruption but rather, however disturbing and demanding, as the ultimate value. That this has importance for the rounded conduct of our lives at all levels should be plain. But there is one aspect of it which I should much like to mention specifically before I close.

Among the consequences of the wrong that we sometimes do one another is the repercussion of our wrong-doing on ourselves, and the most prominent feature of this—what I should regard as the true meaning of "the penalty of sin"—is the encasement of a person more and more in his own inner life. We cannot take with due regard and seriousness the things we violate—and we cannot therefore heed other people properly when we do them wrong. There sets in in this way a spiritual debility, a sense of inner emptiness often remarked upon, which, if not averted, leads to distortion and a sense of being cast adrift to suffocate in the airless existence of unrelieved privacy. These lead to a dissolution of all that matters in personal existence for which total elimination could perhaps be a merciful release—and some have sought it and so understood their faith. For others there are offered other ways of salvation, costly for God as for man; and while it can hardly come within my proper purpose now to examine these, I should like to close with the suggestion that the reflection of religions on this particular theme has a profound, indeed inescapable, relevance to all major practical concerns. We all have a horror of a pure intrusion of religion into moral and political fields. Confusion and escapism have often been the result of that. But I also hold that, with the understanding which the best attainment of our thought today can provide, nothing matters more for our social and political problems than to understand properly where religion impinges upon them. Alike at the strictly academic level, and in field work and more mundane investigation, in devising the right technique in sociology and anthropology, this matter has importance much greater than is usually thought. In the excruciating ultimate test of practical decision and enterprise, it has a great deal more—and that, from my own point of view, is to put the matter cautiously.

On Value and Human Dignity/

AXEL STERN

The years 1936 and 1946, respectively, saw the first and second editions of two shortish books, each concerned with the whole range of human experience, but written by empirical philosophers of almost diametrically opposed views: A. J. Ayer's pungent and elegant presentation of the Vienna Circle's logical positivism, in his *Language, Truth, and Logic*;[1] and John Macmurray's most succinct statement of his socio-religious empiricism, in his Yale University Terry Lectures, *The Structure of Religious Experience*.[2]

To describe these two very different authors as empiricists is not a verbal trick, but quite proper. Both, indeed, recognise continuous reference to objectively controllable experience as being indispensable and decisive for considering their assertions well founded. Out of 145 pages of text, Ayer discusses, and neatly expedites as non-empirical, ethics and theology or religious knowledge in eighteen (1936) plus two (1946) pages, throwing in (or, rather, out) aesthetics for good measure. Macmurray devotes all his pages to these subjects. The emotive theory of values, in Ayer's and other versions, has had an ample airing; so I shall say little about it. Macmurray's views, on the other hand, have been rather neglected in philosophical circles; and I have chosen a few among the many important points he makes, for presentation and discussion here. Those I have selected concern his belief, which I share despite my having been strongly influenced by the Vienna Circle, that ethics can be given a proper empirical basis.[3]

The Terry Lectures of 1936 are apparently about religion and about religious experience and reflection. It would often be more to the point to use the terms *ethical* and *moral* experience and reflection. Indeed, the total absence of these latter terms would seem to make imperative such replacement in the relevant passages. (The reader will kindly note that, in the following quotations, I have actually made this substitution wherever necessary.)

> If values are either utility-values or intrinsic values . . . what room is there for a third type of value which would be neither the one nor the other? . . . Against the question: "What are we to make of the world?" [with the two, not mutually exclusive answers: "It is for our use" or "for our delight"] we must set the question: "What is the world to make of us?" . . . . We and our attitudes of mind are part of the world. . . . The attitude of mind in which we realize this . . . is the attitude of ethics. . . . The moral attitude actually enlarges the scope of the field. . . . In the field of ethics, each of us appears twice, both as the source of valuation and as the object of valuation. (pp. 24, 26.)

> The primary fact is that part of the world of common experience for each of us is the rest of us. . . . When I deal with things in the world which are not human beings, I can treat them as subject to any valuation which I like to impose. I can either use them or admire them. But if the objects I have to deal with are other people, this is impossible, for . . . all personal relationships are mutual and reciprocal in their very nature. . . . If I adopt an attitude to another person that gives him for me a utility-value merely, . . . the only possible reply he can make is a flat denial. . . . The artistic attitude equally fails to establish satisfactory relations between people. . . . The other person would have value in himself for me. But this would be incompatible with his having a value in himself for himself. . . . What is required in our relations with one another if we are to recognize in practice the essential reciprocity of the relationship, is an attitude which somehow contains both of the other two attitudes while transcending them both. We have to enter into fellowship with one another and so create community. (pp. 28, 29, 30.)

According to Macmurray we can unroll the field of common experience from three different points. It will then offer very different aspects. Indeed, *data* may be *given* (as the dictionary tells us), but they have to be *taken*. And this implies some valuation, whether the data are, as it were, pressed upon us, or whether we have freely given our attention to them (rather than to others). We ascribe to the data of either kind, in so far as we take them up at all, differing degrees of importance and relevance, according to the sort of attitude (in our activity or reflection) that is ours at the time. I should, however, distinguish at least four kinds (leaving out the religious one, which seems to me — except in Macmurray's peculiar use of the term — a somewhat uneasy mixture of the others): the scientific, moral, aesthetic, and economico-utilitarian (technical) attitudes (and, thus, values).

Macmurray identifies science, art, and morals (religion), respectively, with utility-values, intrinsic values, and the transcendance of these two. There is, however, no such coincidence of the first and second groups or classifications of values. Both utility and intrinsic values occur from whichever point we unroll the field of common experience. Further, the religious (or moral) attitude, he says, "contains both [the scientific and the aesthetic] while transcending them both." If one asks now what sort of *value* corresponds to it, there is no explanation forthcoming, only the term "religious" (or "moral"); but this is the *explicandum*.

Four Attitudes Towards Experience

Somewhat to clarify the suggested four-fold value approach to the "world of common experience," considerations about the feasibility of neglecting one or the other may be helpful.

(i) Truth is a value that is inescapably all-pervasive as the other values are not. Factual (in the "natural" and "social" sciences) and formal (in mathematics and logic) truths cannot be ignored by anyone without him putting his very existence (and possibly that of those who depend on him) at risk. The law of gravitation cannot sensibly be dismissed as a silly Italian (because of Galileo) or English (because of Newton) prejudice.

Whoever thinks, aims by that very fact at thinking validly, i.e. truly, both as concerns form (logic) and content (facts).[4] That is why truth is a value that is irrecusable.

(ii) To ignore economic-utilitarian values makes an agent or his efforts inefficient or even quite ineffectual. Yet people who live and like a quiet, rather withdrawn existence will rarely be affected by being and being considered inefficient in most respects. On the other hand, an economic-utilitarian selection and assessment of facts and the ensuing actions are frequently alleged to be "realistic" and "value-free"; their practitioners tend to assimilate them to science. (Perhaps this has contributed to Macmurray's classification.) Science qua science endeavors to search for, and establish, its truths without allowing moral, aesthetic, or socio-economic and political values to interfere. As far as it succeeds in this, it is called "value-free." Economic-utilitarian values are, by their very nature, wholly secondary ones, means to ends. All the same, people may well delight just in being efficient. They choose many (thought not all) of their "ends" according to the efficiency they can display in achieving them. As for the so-called realist, i.e. the opportunist, he espouses whichever end appears to him most likely to succeed. With regard to practical economics: it aims at the material flourishing of the community or, at any rate, of a particular part of it. This can hardly be called "value-free." It affects the whole community and its acceptance by all members cannot be taken for granted, especially not when the expected material prosperity seems likely to benefit them somewhat selectively.

(iii) The ignoring of aesthetic values is, alas, widespread without at all endangering the aesthetically insensitive. This topic will, however, not be pursued here since aesthetics lies outside the theme of this essay. Also, the existence and distinctness of aesthetic values or, rather, value attributions is hardly disputed by anyone.

(iv) Moral insensitivity leads to sanctions against the insensitive by his society, that is, if he happens seriously enough to contravene its accepted rules, i.e. its conventions, its positive morality, or its legal code. But this is a socio-psychological fact, not a moral argument. Macmurray speaks of "satisfactory relations" and says: "if we are to recognize in practice the essential reciprocity . . . ." However true and persuasive this may be (and the emotivists would readily agree about its persuasiveness), it begs the question. Does everyone agree as to what are satisfactory relations? Does everyone wish to recognize the "essential reciprocity"? Is not the reciprocity essential only for said "satisfactory relations"? It is undoubtedly a fact that human beings are interrelated and mutually dependent, that man is essentially social (*zoon politikón*), viz. that he would never have become what we call a *human* being without intercourse with other human beings, and that such intercourse is indispensable for at least a fair part of each person's life. Yet, as far as Macmurray's *argument* goes, we may use others merely for their utility-value or may take them (though not all of them) merely as "objects for our delight" or adoration, *without being inconsistent.*

No ethical argument can, of course, be compelling in the sense of actually forcing a person to act in accordance with its conclusion, without ceasing to be an *ethical* argument. (Menaces or legal enforcements are, indeed, not ethical arguments.) What it *can* do (and what Macmurray's is not successful in doing nor really intended to do) is to show that the — general or particular — attitude or (kind of) action of a person is inconsistent with the value or values that he actually holds (or, possibly even, cannot but hold). This is what I hope to show concerning the non-recognition of human dignity.

RESPECT FOR PERSONS: A HISTORICAL FACT?

The problem of human dignity, not in the sense of that of human beings *versus* that of other animals, but in the sense of the dignity of each human being as a person, has come to the fore with the rise of mercantilism and capitalism and an increasing individual self-awareness. A very clear manifestation of it can be found in the assertion of the protestant reformers that each Christian has to face his God directly and without mediation. The most explicit proclamation of human dignity can perhaps be seen in Kant's second formulation of his "categorical imperative": "Act in such a way that you treat humanity, in your own person as well as in the person of any other, never merely as a means but always also as an end."[5]

For Kant, morality (i.e. rational morality) cannot be but categorical and he identifies it with the one and only "categorical imperative" (though he gives several formulations of it, whose derivation from its basic form is perhaps not always quite convincing). The fact that his arguments constitute only an explication and development of this, including the assumption of an intrinsic purposefulness of Nature, but not a proof or justification, shows that it is "absolutely presupposed" by him. I am applying here the useful concept that R. G. Collingwood puts forward in his *Essay on Metaphysics*.[6] All statements, all questions presuppose others; a presupposition is called "absolute" when statements etc. are justified with reference to it, or invalidated for their not being consonant with it, but which itself cannot be justified by, or derived from, anything else; "true" and "false" are thus not applicable to it. Ayer as well as the other emotivists can be said to endorse the categorical character of ethics, but to treat it as an assertion. No wonder they discover that it cannot be either deduced or justified. From this they conclude, bewitched as they are by Kant's "moral = categorical" (which also mirrors most people's psychological attitude), not that a rational morality is not categorical, but that there cannot be any ethical statements proper. "I want the moon; but since I can't have it, I won't have *any* light at night."

However sadly human dignity is ignored in the practice of Western societies, it is, while perhaps not an absolute presupposition, certainly an integral part of their positive morality. This is shown, for example, by the very fact that even the worst offenders pay lip-service to it. Indeed, just as lying logically presupposes the background of truthfulness, so hypocrisy is the implicit admission of a prevailing moral standard. However, I cannot feel satisfied with the mere assertion of this socio-psychological fact, nor can I take human dignity for granted as an absolutely presupposed value (or as the object of a categorical imperative). In order to make an attempt at justifying the recognition of human dignity, a further clarification of the concept of value seems a useful preliminary.

We owe to Galileo, Descartes, and then Locke the distinction of "primary" and "secondary" qualities. Colours, sounds, tastes, and smells were not inherent qualities of the objective world, but arose from the senses being affected by the primary qualities of solidity, extension, figure, motion and rest, and number. This distinction has since been shown to be untenable. Yet, the notion of secondary qualities seems to me a fruitful one for elucidating that of values. Indeed, the fact that values arise presupposes sentiment thinking agents, for instance and in particular, human beings. Since these latter have a language, and a reflective and thus conceptualised one at that, this presupposes their essential sociality. Values arise because we are in conscious interrelation with the world around us, be it human or non-human. We do things and abstain from doing others, we affect our surroundings, as they also affect us and as we react towards that. And we are conscious of most of all this — prospectively (i.e. we intend, have purposes, fears, etc.), at the time, and/or retrospectively. Being human necessarily implies valuing.

So, whatever Plato believed, worth or value cannot meaningfully be said to exist or subsist in itself; it must pertain to something. Neither does it inhere in things as things; it essentially requires a consciousness as a referent, though usually only by implication. Here G. E. Moore, for one, held a different view when he maintained, concerning two worlds, one exceedingly beautiful, the other disgustingly ugly, both of which were, however, quite inaccessible to any possible visitor or contemplator, that it was *not* "irrational to hold that it is better that the beautiful world should exist, than the one that is ugly."[7] What Moore failed to see (perhaps because it was not relevant to his objection to Sidgwick, where the passage occurs) was that "beautiful" and "ugly," and our preferring the former to the latter, make sense only thanks to Moore's and his readers' *thinking* about them. Values are *secondary* qualities: there is no value without a potential or actual *valuer*; and a valuer attaches value *to* something.

As for truth as a value, there are a number of dissentient voices nowadays, excising it from the classical triad: the True, the Good, the Beautiful (with their opposites). Truth, it was noted, is all-pervasive in a way the others are not. There is also the hotly disputed transition from "is" statements to "ought" statements, the latter being identified with ethics and aesthetics. Yet, whatever may be said to set "true" apart from the others, this term (and its opposite, "false") is meaningless unless applied *by* a thinking being *to* some belief etc. entertained by him or some other such being. The earth revolves on its axis and round the sun, whether or not there is anyone to observe it; but the *statement* is true and its negation false only if there is someone to make it (aloud or silently, in writing or otherwise), though he may make it *about* the present or *about* the (though not unlimitedly far) past or future. If these remarks are thought to be trivial, well, so they probably are. But the point needs remembering.

Now, when do we attribute value (*viz.* positive or negative value) to something? When in our feeling or thinking we are concerned about it, however indirectly, or believe others thus to be concerned — whether or not we expect it to affect our or their actual interests. Putting it negatively: when it does not leave us strictly indifferent. There are, I suggested above, four different but not mutually exclusive attitudes towards the field of common experience and, thereby, four kinds of value. I now want to consider two other ways of looking at values (quite compatible with the first) and distinguish (1) between *subjective* and *objective,* and (2) between *intrinsic* and *instrumental* values.

(1) If, and so fas as, a valuation is, and is considered to be, one of personal preference or aversion, an expression of taste and of likes or dislikes (even when they happen to be shared by others and, in this sense, be general), then such a value is called "*subjective.*" If, and so far as, a valuation implies a claim to being universally valid for all people who are, in all relevant respects, similarly placed (even when only one person happens to make this valuation), then such a value is called "*objective.*" We may note that subjective and objective values may, but need not, be attributed simultaneously to one and the same object.

(2) If, and so far as, something is believed to serve (or to

prevent or inhibit the achievement of) a further purpose, it is said to have or be invested with positive (or negative) *"instrumental"* or *"utility"* value. If, and so far as, something is positively (or negatively) appreciated for its own sake, for what it is, was, will be in itself, it is said to have or be invested with positive (or negative) *"intrinsic"* value. Again, we may note that instrumental and intrinsic values may, but need not, be attributed to one and the same object; in fact, this goes for any combination of subjective and objective, instrumental and intrinsic values. With reference to the latter pair, however, it should be further noted that whatever instrumental value is attributed to something must, in the end, derive from and depend on the intrinsic value attributed to something *else*. It is also important to realise that, consequently, attribution of intrinsic values is indispensable for instrumental values being attributed to anything at all. Yet, that to which we attribute intrinsic value at one time, may lose this value for us; it may also additionally have or gain instrumental value or values (since any one thing may be invested with any number of instrumental values); lastly, from having been an end for us, it may become a means to some further end.

Concerning intrinsic values, someone might raise the following objection: "When I like something for its own sake, does this not mean that I like it *because* it gives me pleasure or delight, that I care for it, cherish it, keep it, do it, make it, foster it, or contemplate it *in order to* get enjoyment from it?" The expressions "because" and "in order to" seem to point to instrumental value. This is, however, a misapprehension due to grammatical usage. Yet what underlies the question (and, perhaps, even the grammatical usage) is perfectly sound. It is precisely what has been stressed already, namely, that nothing can be of value nor, therefore, of intrinsic value, unless it be *for someone*. To attribute (positive) intrinsic value to something *means* to enjoy, to like, to cherish it for its own sake, to delight in the very thought of its past, present, or future existence, and so on.

As for people (and they are the central issue in this paper), if they have only (positive) intrinsic value for us,[8] we make them thereby into objects of worship or of mere aesthetic appreciation, putting them, as it were, into a glass case, on a pedestal, congealing them into waxen images for our adoration. All this makes personal interrelationships impossible. It also impoverishes our view and understanding of people, since we are likely to disregard, or blind ourselves to, the non-idolisable parts of their personality. On the other hand, if other people have only instrumental value for us, we make them into mere tools, animated machines for our use and at our disposal. This makes personal interrelationships no less impossible. Here the impoverishment of our view and understanding of people is even more marked, since their use-value consists only in whatever function we require them to fulfil. Both attitudes imply the ignoring or denying of human dignity. So the two main questions of this essay have now to be tackled: first, What is meant by "human dignity"? and second, Are there rational (not simply persuasive) grounds for respecting it?

THE CONCEPT OF HUMAN DIGNITY

As a first formulation let us say: *Human dignity consists in our recognising that each human being, including ourselves, has intrinsic value and is a valuer in his own right.*

The term "recognising" means in this context "attributing intrinsic value to." The first formulation can, then, be developed into this somewhat more elaborate formulation: Human dignity consists in our attributing intrinsic value to both

(i) each person's having intrinsic value for himself and to his being himself a valuer; and

(ii) the kind of relationship that thereby becomes possible between people, viz. personal interrelationship. (A time-honoured formulation of this is: "Love your neighbour as yourself," which implies, be it noted, that you love yourself, too.)

Assuming the first formulation to be acceptable, it has to be shown that the second one, especially point (ii), is a valid expansion of it. If we attribute intrinsic value to something, this means that we wish to maintain and foster it and to ensure that it is not damaged or diminished in any way; that in fact we will, as far as we can, prevent or counteract such damage. Now, according to the first formulation, we attribute intrinsic value, not simply to other people, but to other people's attributing intrinsic value to themselves as human, that is, social, thinking and feeling beings. And, since we are not extraneous observers but human beings ourselves, this necessarily includes our attributing intrinsic value to our mutual relations with them.

This, in its turn, implies point (i) and, more specifically, our recognition of other people's freedom of choice, in other words, of their autonomy in valuation. Such recognition amounts, in particular, to our abstaining, as far as circumstances allow, from attempts at forcing them directly or indirectly to change their views, attitudes, or behaviour, i.e. their attribution of positive or negative values. (This is also one ground for considering lies, and thus certain kinds of education, propaganda and advertising, to be immoral as offending against human dignity.) In short, if we respect their human dignity, we want people freely to be what they can be and genuinely want to be. It is not contrary to this, but in perfect consonance with it, that we may try to convince people when we believe them to be in error, though remaining fully aware that it may be we ourselves who are in error or who mistakenly attribute to them purposes that are not theirs. In other words, we shall be tolerant, not from indifference, but from interest in the full personality of others and in their autonomy.

Just as the recognition of other people's freedom is an integral part of our recognition of their dignity, so does our own dignity include the consciousness of our own freedom of choice, the awareness that our valuations are our own and that, fully to be such, they must be neither arbitrary nor coerced. (This implies the moral rejection of self-deception, which is parallel to that of lying to others.)

People's autonomy is part of their dignity and should, therefore, be respected if human dignity is recognised. Yet I said above: "as far as circumstances allow": this requires spelling out. Those among us, such as adults who have grown up in unfavourable conditions or as young children anywhere, who are as yet unable validly to think in terms of equality with others (whether they take themselves to be superior or inferior human beings), do require some assistance or guidance or even direction to achieve a genuine freedom of choice. (The genuineness of such freedom resides in the ability of an unprejudiced consideration of the possibilities that are actually open.) Such assistance or guidance or direction does not ignore these people's human dignity. For it stems from, and — to be what it is intended to be — is limited by, the concern to allow them the clear awareness and achievement of their own human dignity.

However, in most actual cases of interference with (grown) people's autonomy and freedom of choice (and, by repercussion, with the growing people's as well) we notice little or no preoccupation with human dignity. What we find most often is a social organisation that hampers or makes impossible, for a large number of its members, the achievement of their full humanity and human dignity. Then, circumstances may make these people realise the inferior human status that such a society allots to them. With such awareness may come moves by which they will try to remould or even overthrow the prevailing socio-political order.

Since the discussion concerns *human* dignity, I assume the equality of all humans in this respect and shall not examine at length whether any group of people might validly be considered as either humanly inferior or humanly superior to the rest. Race or sex, physique or intelligence, birth or occupation, creed or class are in this context irrelevant; this is my thesis. The onus of proving the relevance of such differences lies upon those who want to assert it.

Still, a short reference to George Orwell's *1984*[9] may illustrate one aspect of this issue. Big Brother's attempt to subjugate all citizens' valuations to his own are carried, in Winston Smith's case, to the length of making W. S. finally accept with conviction that 2 and 2 make 5 whenever Big Brother says so. This result cannot, like all previous abasements and abandonments, be achieved by means of persuasion, menaces or suffering: it requires W. S.'s total nervous breakdown, which destroys in him the rational normative system itself. Though W. S. could, at that stage, still fulfill the role of a mere animal, Big Brother has lost all interest in him. There is indeed no imaginable further triumph or possible victory. Big Brother has, as it were, overshot his target; for he has deprived himself of an equal (which in Big Brother's eyes W.S. was, despite the latter's very inferior position), since W. S. is no longer a human being proper.

I shall, then, take it that we all belong to the same *moral* species, whatever our individual or group differences. This view is in marked contrast to the practice (and its rationalisations) of some of our contemporaries, but more notably to the tenets of Plato and Aristotle. The latter, in particular, avers that "it is impossible to practice virtue (*areté*) if one lives the life of a worker or labourer."[10] I shall, on the contrary, assume no fundamental dichotomy between thought and action, between reflection and manual work. The purely contemplative life appears to me rather as one form of self-estrangement. Thinking divorced from doing is drained of meaning; doing divorced from thinking is mere drill, blind instinct, or aimless agitation. If this is accepted, then to be moral and, for that matter, morally autonomous is not, nor can it be, a question of intellectual endowment or cleverness.

THE VALUE OF HUMAN DIGNITY

Human beings are conscious, feeling, and thinking agents and, in consequence, are necessarily valuers. Are there any values or, less generally, any ethical values that they *have* to hold lest they be inconsistent? More particularly, is human dignity such a value? This is, I suggested earlier, the only line of argument by which morality and moral assertions can, on purely rational grounds, be supported. For such objective, i.e. rationally conclusive, value attributions to be also motivationally effective, they must be (or become) subjective as well. However, problems of motivation should, where necessary, be pointed out in philosophical discussions, but they do not belong to their subject matter.

Hobbes's assumptions about man seem to me, as to most people, mistaken or, at any rate, distortingly partial. Yet his *mode* of argument is sound, in contrast with that of the majority of moral philosophers. We are, he says in substance, all wholly selfish — or, in terms of the present essay: the only thing to which each of us can and does attribute intrinsic value is his own life and its security — so-called immoral behaviour is unenlightened, short-sighted, and stupid; and the immoral person is inconsistent as between what he is actually bringing about and his self-interest.

Thus, what I have to ask now is: (i) Why and how does the non-recognition of human dignity in others empty our lives of what we actually value, being incompatible with the self-respect that we insist on having? and (ii) Why and how can we not consistently make our own worth depend entirely or mainly on our value for others? The two issues are opposite sides of the same coin. To anticipate: he who only uses others diminishes himself; he who makes himself into a mere instrument of his god diminishes the latter as well as himself.

(i) The authoritarian who subjugates others may do so in his family or, politically, in his party, province or state; he may be a schoolmaster with his pupils, a factory director with his workers, an officer with his men, a commissar with those he controls, a priest with his flock, or . . . and so on. On this score such a man makes his worth depend so far on his power over others, whom he transforms into tools, viz. tools for proving and aggrandising his power. In fact, however, he has involved himself in a vicious circle. Indeed, there cannot be approval or recognition under compulsion. When I myself turn the handle of the applause machine, obviously nobody applauds me. The more effectively I reduce others to the class of objects, the more I dehumanise myself, for I surround myself with puppets instead of living with human beings. The more successful I fancy I am, the less successful I am in fact.

The ruthlessly ambitious man may hold that those who allow themselves to be squashed and made into his tools or puppets, "do not deserve any better." This defence is not sound. In the first place, what has just been said about the authoritarian applies here as well; for ambition and competition logically presuppose a public and competitors. Among the people he has not (yet) beaten, those who in their careers have been considerate to others will have no esteem for him. As for those of his own kind — whom he may impress — a second and more important argument applies. A ruthless attitude to people amounts to an actual admission of one's own inferiority. One acts as if one were incapable of being successful if one had to deal honestly with equals and had to counter in a fair way their objections and opposition, or even to recognise their superior qualities (except in ruthlessness, intrigue and cunning). So we say to the big bully who knocks about a small boy: "Pick on someone your own size."

On the other hand, it has to be admitted that, where a basic inequality between human beings is taken for granted, that is, where human beings are held to be of fundamentally different kinds or species, the preceding arguments do, to that extent, not apply. Indeed, we cannot be said necessarily to degrade ourselves if we use oxen without attributing intrinsic value to them or to their valuings. As to the relations among the members of the "oxen using" group, of course, the arguments hold good.

(ii) Taking the reverse situation, we have the person who divests himself of his human dignity and makes himself into an implement of another's thoughts, will, and actions. He degrades not only himself, but also the other, whom he thinks he exalts, in a way similar to that of the authoritarian's actually degrading himself. Indeed, in so far as we have no intrinsic value for ourselves and our valuings are not our own but subordinate to those of another or others, whatever we do ourselves cannot, in our own eyes, be of value, including more particularly our value judgements. Thus our attribution of value to another is, of necessity, proportionately reduced or made worthless. To put this point somewhat paradoxically: the recognition of a person's superiority (in some respect or several) is meaningful only among equals.

It further follows that a person's saying: "My intrinsic value for myself is nil, I am a mere nothing" is self-cancelling (though it may be perfectly sincere). As will be clear from the earlier discussion, it is not justifiable to deny their human dignity to the self-abased; there are, on the contrary, good grounds for trying to awaken or strengthen their own awareness of it. The obsolescent species of the blindly adoring wife, for instance, who makes her husband out to be a faultless idol, deprives him of the intelligent and discriminating encouragement and approval that he may need.

For if whatever he does is approved by her because it is he who does it, such approval is quite worthless and, with it, also his actions — that is, in so far as his wife is concerned, since she has made herself into a cypher. Still, there are quite a few people who are apparently full of themselves but, in actual fact, are so unsure of their own worth that they like and seek from others such indiscriminate approbation and praise.

Human dignity is essentially social and based on the necessary interdependence of human beings. Basically and inevitably we are of instrumental value to one another. While the strength of this interdependence depends on the smaller and larger communities of which we are members, its extension has, in modern times, become global. Since our lives and activities are meaningful only in so far as we have purposes and attribute intrinsic value to things, human dignity is central. It asserts the implicit or explicit reciprocity of all *rationally valid* human relations; to ignore it, be it in oneself or in others, constitutes a contradiction between the aim and the result of one's behaviour.

The human dignity of the self, our self-respect, implies that we hold ourselves morally responsible for what we do or omit doing. In fact, this follows from our rationality, the recognition of which constitutes part of this our dignity. Thus the acknowledgement of our guilt, when we have actually made a mistake or acted wrongly or harmfully, is rational, i.e. in accordance with, and not offending against, our human dignity. So, clearly, are our efforts to remedy the situation we have brought about, and our acceptance of such consequential actions as others of our community or society may validly take against us. A very important issue, which, however, can only be pointed out but not dealt with here, is the socio-economic-political one: When is the human dignity of people qua members of a given organization (e.g. a State) or qua outsiders (such as foreigners, or citizens of another country in a state of war with the first) respected or offended against? This problem can be properly understood and the situations assessed only by reference to the moral acceptability of said organisation and its institutions and actions, and of international relations (peaceful or otherwise) in general.

Human dignity, as a central moral concept, is a relative late-comer, as are those of moral autonomy, with which it is closely connected, and the "equality of all men," from which both have sprung. The *dignity* attached to certain *positions* in the tribe, community, city, or state, on the other hand, is as old as the differentiation of roles and functions within human groupings. The latter sort of dignity is often taken for the former; and it may not be easy or even possible neatly to distinguish between them in any given case. Further, the notions of what is and what is not compatible with one's dignity are, sometimes widely, at variance as from one period, one people or nation, one class or profession to another. The problems connected with these conceptions of dignity, however, do not belong to the present context. Lastly, one could mention that there are some people who "stand on their dignity." This has always struck me as a strange place for one's dignity: under one's feet.

Footnotes

[1] A. J. Ayer, *Language, Truth, and Logic* (London: Victor Gollancz; New York: Dover, 1st ed. 1936; 2d ed. 1946).

[2] John Macmurray, *The Structure of Religious Experience* (London: Faber and Faber, 1st ed. 1936, 2d ed. 1946; reprinted at Hamden, Conn.: Archon Books, 1971).

[3] See, for instance, my *The Science of Freedom* (London: Longmans, 1969).

[4] See my "Truth—A New Approach," *Proceedings of the Aristotelian Society* 65 (1964–65): 99–122.

[5] Immanuel Kant, *Grundlegung zur Metaphysik der Sitten* (Riga, 1785, pp. 66–67 (Akademie edition, p. 429).

[6] R. G. Collingwood, *Essay on Metaphysics* (Oxford and New York: Oxford University Press, 1940).

[7] G. E. Moore, *Principia Ethica,* art. 50 (Cambridge: At the University Press, 1903), pp. 83–84.

[8] If the intrinsic value that we attribute to people is negative, we make them into objects of pure abomination. (Instances of kinds of action to which most people attribute negative intrinsic value are sheer cruelty and the judicial execution of the innocent.) Since the discussion is now concerned with human dignity, the term "value" (unless otherwise stated) is henceforth understood in the more usual way, that is, as "positive value."

[9] George Orwell, *1984* (New York: Harcourt, Brace, World, 1949).

[10] *Politics,* III 1278a.

Global Famine and the Sense of Justice/

BASIL O'LEARY

"This sense of justice," writes John Macmurray, "implies an actual society in which a norm of co-operation has already been established, and which has become habitual. The fact that it works without outcry from people who feel unjustly treated is sufficient guarantee that it is felt to be generally fair and reasonably just."[1] But as never before in human history, an outcry of anguish is being heard in global society. Nearly 500 million persons, most of them children, are close to starvation. Tens of thousands die each week. Ten to twelve million are expected to die of starvation in the next year. And world population grows at a rate of 75 million a year.

Even among those who are not suffering the horrors of famine there is an increasingly loud outcry. Robert Heilbroner, a social scientist, asks, "Is there hope for man?" And he answers his own question: "The outlook for man, I believe, is painful, difficult, perhaps desperate, and the hope that can be held out for his future prospect seems very slim indeed."[2] And John Passmore, a philosopher, says, "I write out of a sense of alarm. . . . men cannot go on living as they have been living on the biosphere."[3]

Malthusian conditions of scarcity are nothing new to mankind, but what is new is the moral problematic that we now face. When pestilence, famine, and war were altogether unmanageable, as unforseeable as they were ineluctable, and—most important of all—essentially local catastrophes, one's sense of justice was not outraged even though one's religious convictions might well be exploded. One did not blame feudalism for the black death. But the present global crisis is a moral crisis as well as an ecological one, since our society not only has small but real reserves of resources—such as midwestern wheat fields—but also the technology—principally that of economic technique—to mitigate if not to eliminate the suffering of men and women in other lands by redistributing the commodities of our farms and factories in accord with our sense of justice. This sense "may be confused, insensitive and poorly developed. But it is the only pragmatic standard available," Macmurray says.[4] A pragmatic standard, however, is inadequate of itself; in what follows I shall argue that it requires a corrective which, while not independent of action, is a reflective grasp of rightness in social decisions. This grasp of rightness is what has traditionally, somewhat rhetorically, and perhaps not a little misleadingly been called natural law.

COMMUNITY AND SOCIETY

The relation of community is one of friendship which is prior to and founds the common purposes of society. It is the realm of direct relationships of persons, each spontaneously and generously promoting the existence of others. Its original manifestation is in the unity of the family, but through increasing size and complexity of the family group is extended to the tribe, nation, or the planet itself. From this ultimate bond, as will be seen, flow convictions as to the dignity of man, the right to livelihood, the care of those less endowed for market competition and those whose special abilities deserve public subsidization. Its unity is symbolized, one way or another, in terms of piety or patriotism.[5]

Society, on the other hand, is the organization of the community in virtue of the specific functions and roles by which individuals can contribute to the welfare of the group. Society, in this view, is not organic, not teleological in an instinctual sense, nor is it an evolutionary process, but it is *intentional,* that is, a network of contractual relationships that efficiently achieve a hierarchy of common purposes. The market is, then a prime instrument of the community, or as Macmurray says,

> Broadly speaking, this negative aspect is economic. But it is
> the negative aspect of a society of persons, and is, therefore,

intentional. It is an intentional cooperation in work, that is, action directed upon the world-as-means, to the corporate production and distribution of the means of personal life in society. This cooperation in work establishes a nexus of indirect relations between all the members of the co-operating group, irrespective of their personal relations, whether these are positive or negative or non-existent. Such relations are not relations of persons as persons, but only as workers; they are relations of the functions which each person performs in the co-operative association; and if this aspect of the personal is abstracted, and considered in isolation, every person is identified with his function. He *is* a miner, or a tinsmith, or a doctor, or a teacher.[6]

This economic aspect of society is purely pragmatic; it aims to produce the greatest amount of goods and services with the least expenditure of effort and resources—for the enhancement of the lives of the persons of the community. In itself, the economic system for cooperation in production and exchange has no reference to justice and freedom, its unity being one of functions, not persons. However, the rules governing this activity are always to be found safeguarding the personal rights of all participants and limiting the arbitrary use of power. Through the law of contracts, for example, a person can specify the limits of his obligations to another and effectively free himself from further involvement.

Economist Kenneth Boulding aptly makes the same distinction in terms of "responsibility for" and "responsibility to." When the object of responsibility is someone for whom we care, then it is a "for" relation, a relation of love. "Responsibility to" is a power relation, in which performance is required at the risk of loss. What causes the market to survive as a social institution lies in its power to persuade those related to it that it "pays" them to continue the relationship. "It must attract workers by offering them at least as good wages and conditions of work as they can get elsewhere. It must attract customers by offering them goods as good and cheap as they can get elsewhere."[7] In the competitive market, it is the ever-present *elsewhere* that effectively limits power.

This dimension of society with its atomistic, isolated units of economic force who rationally construct and maintain structures for cooperation, is also, of course, the domain of economic science. This positive knowledge is concerned with the relation of one thing to another, of factors of production rather than persons, of wages determined by supply and demand rather than by criteria for fairness. But, there remains the relationship of the economically efficient *society* to the persons of the *community*.

The question is, then, how does the community discover the good that mediates scarcity, a prime characteristic of every society? Since it seems to be an economic truism that all scarcity must be handled through some kind of competition—this includes violence, status, class, the free-market—discrimination inevitably follows. Who is favored in the distribution of goods and services depends on the kind of competition that operates. At the root of the choice of institutions that express the preferred form of competition lies a sense of justice informed by some understanding of natural law.

A Sense of Justice and Natural Law

But is there some ultimate test to decide whether a society's sense of justice is an adequate one? After all, mere consensus expressing the popular will can condone the worst tyranny, as history has recently shown, and on the theoretical level, voluntaristic positivism would hold that any set of existing laws and institutions is the best simply because it is. Absolutely speaking, no determinate rule or standard exists whereby the sense of justice might be judged, or the validity of its implications in bringing economic life to express the values of the community challenged.

In the physical sciences, experimental laws, because based on observational evidence, can have a life of their own independently of the theories that provide them with explanations of more or less generality; they can and have survived the eventual demise of a succession of theories. For example, Millikan's famous oil drop experiment, from which it is known that all electrical charges are integral multiples of a certain elementary charge, is interpreted differently in pre-quantum theory, in Bohr's theory, and in the post-Bohr theories. Such experimental laws are intelligible in themselves regardless of the special technical structures of differing universes of explanation.

In very much the same fashion, the lived-reality of the natural law—whether expressed by Sophocles' *Antigone*, St. Paul, or Edmond Cahn in his "sense of injustice"—exercises the same function independently of the *world*, or theory, which grounds it intellectually. Its basic thrust is an act of faith that the human community will not be overwhelmed by the untoward events and forces thrown up in the course of its history; that human reason can discover an ordering intelligibility that will give meaning to its communal existence, onserving and promoting it; that there is some Absolute conferring legitimacy to law and providing standards for an ordered administration of justice. Whatever the source of its authority, or how it is made known to men, or how it is given expression, natural law through the centuries has been a light piercing the darkness of polyvalent irrationality threatening human existence.

Whenever there is an appeal to the "court of reason" or to "what reasonable men generally recognize" as ultimate standards justifying civil law and human conduct, the validity of such argument, for its possessors at least, is not truly human or "natural" until it becomes part of an integral world vision from which it draws its absoluteness, universality, immutability. That is, the ultimate defense against the arbitrary and the relative must be verified as "natural," and this is somehow a participation in a Logos or ultimately rational scheme of things. However, the course of the history of natural law theory reveals a diversity of horizons that have been urged to account for its natural function: from Stoic pantheism, to Christians sharing in the Divine Intellect, and to H. L. A. Hart's "survival of the legal order."

Human nature does have a structure, a profound inclination, and a necessary end which give rise to the natural law of its operation. It is simple: to allow other men "to be" (and, paradoxically, become a person oneself) and actively to promote our mutual existence through a detached and unrestricted inquiry as to the goods that preserve the dialogal relation of the community. It is important to recognize the "language shift" in speaking of the structure of the nature to be conformed to. In a sense, the structure of man awake to the needs of the community is to have no structure, that is, to be open, creatively attentive to the rational requirements of this historical moment. As J. de Finance once observed, the ground of ethics lies in reason's conformity to itself, not as nature but as reason, *ratio rationaliter se exercens*.[8]

In the process of decision and actual carrying out of projects and their instrumentalities, whether as an individual, choosing, for example, to help retarded children, or a state, facing the problem of rising population and limited resources, each successive step gives rise to questions as to how best respond to one's commitment. Only through careful participation in the action itself does one phase after another reveal its incompleteness, only to raise further questions for the economist and the decision-maker. Practical affairs on all levels have a self-correcting measure as reason actualizes its own immanent norms, proposing hypotheses and verifying them in the concrete unfolding of the here and now.[9]

The energy for moral originality in the sense of justice streams from the community, the personal level of the *I-Thou* relation; it is operative, according to man's nature, as reason actively questioning how to preserve through time this super-existence of personal communion.

If natural law were conceived as a static code, or nature as an object, then, indeed, it would be incompatible with creativity; but natural law as the ground of human action, like metaphysics as the ultimate grasp of being, begins not with a concept or a proposition, but with a lived-performance: the acts of questioning and discussion done by a free society within the dialectic of community, making concrete decisions for the sake of the other. It is, in short, law-creating law.

Norms that do emerge as the community seeks to be reasonable inevitably concern the most common activities of man, those having to do with sex, life and death, property and contracts, and —often omitted because unformulated though always found in any group—loyalty, cooperation, reliability. Of course, these formulated norms are not themselves *natural law*, any more than the measured fall of any existent body could express formally and exactly Newton's axioms of motion. The question persists, how does the community achieve certitude that any given normative conceptualization is a correct actualization of natural law? Since what is sought is a practical knowledge measuring action, the living body and the science of medicine have some pertinence here. Just as the living organism reveals a constant tendency toward health, repelling infections and repairing wounds through a spontaneous mobilization of its chemical and physiological processes, so does the human community spontaneously inquire and act to insure its survival. The knowledge of natural law, then, grows and is validated in a manner analogous to the practice of medicine. As the rules of physical and medical practice are better known with the development of the medical sciences, so the conditions of social health are better known, the sense of justice takes on more authentically human shape, as the sciences of social life—economics, sociology, political science—develop. No more certitude can be asked for the social order than for the body.

From the introduction of the Brandeis Brief in judicial procedure to today's rapidly developing economics, as well as the other social sciences, there is a sharper awareness that society can profitably be treated as an object. From the observed regularities of communities securing material goods and services, governing themselves, and mutually adjusting to cultural and racial differences, general theories can be constructed, the implications of which become useful data for authority in fashioning legislation or making decisions and policies that shape society's sense of justice. The analogy of the social sciences being to the natural law what the medical sciences are to the doctor is true only in a *material* way. The structures and necessities of markets, the theories about the distribution of political power, for example, are part of the past because they express a relation between objects themselves empirically verified, but whose significance as operative principles in effecting justice is found only in their dialectical relation to the future in the judgment to be made in the present. That is, natural law justice, looking to the present needs of persons, treats questions of efficiency and material survival as secondary and ministerial to human values. The sense of justice expresses the *values* of the community through the *structures* of society. For example, tariffs and minimum wage laws are economically inefficient; yet in certain political situations, legislators can find no other means of achieving national welfare or helping impoverished workers.

All the expectations of invariance and necessity, traditionally sought for in the natural law, find their fulfillment in the "filled present" of the moment of decision which unites the "given" of the past and the destiny of the future. In response to the call of its ultimate horizon, mediated always concretely through the persons of the community, men's reason achieves a heightened creativity in deciding what to do now. Paul Ramsey correctly situates natural law's novelty in the historicity of man: "Knowledge of natural law is no longer a matter of reflecting upon essential human nature in abstraction from variable factual conditions and social relationships. Knowledge by connaturality, congeniality, inclination arises only vis-à-vis quite concrete conditions of fact."[10]

Natural law, then, in the light of today's understanding of personal and social reality, is nothing else than the assurance that man has of living in a meaningful course of history and that through his unrestricted power of questioning can come to solutions for the events encountered in society. Any procedures that promote personal creativity, free inquiry, and genuine discussion are natural law approaches toward a sense of justice guiding the ever-evolving course of society.

Footnotes

[1] John Macmurray, *Persons in Relation* (London, 1961), p. 202.
[2] Robert Heilbroner, "The Human Prospect," *The New York Review of Books* 20 (January 24, 1974), 21-22.
[3] John Passmore, *Man's Responsibility for Nature* (New York, 1974), p. ix.
[4] *Persons in Relation*, p. 203.
[5] John Macmurray, *Conditions of Freedom* (London, 1949), p. 85.
[6] *Persons in Relation*, p. 186.
[7] Kenneth Boulding, "The Principle of Personal Responsibility," in *Beyond Economics* (Ann Arbor, 1970), p. 213.
[8] Joseph de Finance, *Existence et Liberté* (Paris, 1955), p. 86.
[9] Bernard Lonergan, *Insight* (New York, 1957), pp. 174, 234.
[10] Paul Ramsey, *Nine Modern Moralists* (Englewood Cliffs, N. J., 1962), p. 220.

The Personal Universe/

ALBERT H. NEPHEW

John Macmurray was born in Scotland in 1891 into a family that he appreciatively characterized as "deeply religious." His parents were keenly interested in mission work, and when his father died without fulfilling his own hope of becoming a missionary, Macmurray attempted to join the missions. But he was not accepted, so in 1913, upon graduating from the University of Glasgow, he moved to Oxford to study philosophy. After only a year there, his studies were interrupted by the First World War. He first considered pacifism, then decided to join the army as a medic, discovered that in practice the medic was a kind of fighting man too, accepted a commission in the Cameron Highlanders, was wounded and sent home; the war ended before he could be sent back. He finished his degree course in 1919.

He began publishing in 1925, with an essay delivered as part of a symposium on aesthetics sponsored by the Aristotelian Society; he continued to deliver papers and responses to papers before the Society until the late 1930's. This was his most prolific period, but he published almost continuously until 1965, when he delivered the Swarthmore Lecture, a partly autobiographical presentation printed under the title *Search for Reality in Religion.* This essay takes up the religious themes of another essay written in the last decade, *Religion, Art and Science* (1961), as well as those of his Terry Lectures at Yale, published as *The Structure of Religious Experience* (1936). But his most significant work, religious or otherwise, is unquestionably his Gifford Lectures of 1953-54.

The commission of a Gifford lecturer—whose prestigious ranks include theologians such as Karl Barth and Rudolf Bultmann as well as philosophers such as A. J. Ayer and Henri Bergson—is to answer the questions: "What contribution does this philosophical study make to the problem of the validity of religious belief? Are there, or are there not, rational grounds for a belief in God?"[1] And although Gifford lecturers have not hesitated to give negative answers to the latter question—Barth said there are grounds but no rational ones; Ayer said there were no grounds at all—the preoccupation of Macmurray's lectures with human rather than divine personhood can give the impression that he has forgotten the basic purpose of the Gifford Lectureship.

But this impression is dispelled in his final chapter, entitled "The Personal Universe," where he shows how the new philosophical standpoint he has been advocating provides rational grounds for believing in God as the Agent whose action the historical world is. God's otherness is a *personal* otherness, and the verification of belief in God is to be found in the differences this belief makes to human action.

However, to appreciate these and his other "theological" conclusions as something more than religious poetry, we must understand the novelty of Macmurray's entire philosophy, which is to say, the creative sweep of the chapters that precede the one just mentioned. Accordingly, I shall try in this essay to develop some of the more important themes of the Gifford Lectures, though I shall not try to be exhaustive. Nor shall I limit myself to that work, although my references to his other writings will be incidental.

THE FORM OF THE PERSONAL

Although the two volumes of the Gifford Lectures are titled separately (*The Self as Agent,* and *Persons in Relation,* respectively), they also bear the joint title *The Form of the Personal*. This indicates the importance for Macmurray of establishing the proper conceptual model or logical form for understanding what is unique to human relationships. The pursuit of such a model began early in his career: in 1928 he called it a logical "schema," in 1933 a "unity pattern," and two years later, in *Creative Society*, he analyzed it as the unity of a positive and a negative element, in which the positive overcomes the negative and the negative is necessary to constitute the positive. Thus love as a positive term must be able to "spend itself," which it cannot do unless someone is in need, need being a negative term. This analysis is expanded in *Self as Agent*, and developed into the anti-dualist thesis that thought is but the negative, supporting element of *action*. Then, in *Persons in Relation*, other positive-negative unities such as fear-love and science-art are taken up, and understood as culminating in the supreme unity of truly personal communion.

Since Descartes, most philosophers have overlooked the logical primacy of action. Both the metaphysical and anti-metaphysical tendencies in modern philosophy have been built on the same foundation, the Cartesian *Cogito*. This fundamentally individualistic metaphysics, centered in the self-as-thinker-and-knower, and logically trapped there, has had a long history of dominance, dating back at least to Plato and Parmenides. This dominating solipsistic idealism, restricted from dealing with most of the facts of the everyday world of practical reality including interpersonal relations and personal action, has invited the charge that it has built not on a solid foundation of experience but on a chimera of contemplation, a non-existent "pure self." Kant's is the epitome of this kind of philosophy, for he postulates a "pure reason" that cannot deal with extra-mental reality and can only accept the existence of action on faith. Even the philosophies which claim to be "empirical," however, are fettered by subjectivism and egocentrism insofar as they work from the *Cogito* standpoint.

The way out of this trap is by means of what Macmurray calls a new Copernican Revolution. Copernicus reversed the understanding of the relation of the earth and the sun; Kant, with his Copernican Revolution, reversed the understanding of the relation of subject and object, making the object dependent on the subject, that is, making knowledge dependent on the categories in the mind of the knower. Macmurray's revolution transcends the realm of pure thought and postulates action as primary in relation to thought by reversing the relation of subject and agent, of knower and doer. Action (personal, intended action) becomes a given, self-evident to the agent who is a person by virtue of interpersonal relations and a knower and thinker through the same mediation. Thought is therefore secondary, serving the ends of action. Macmurray refuses to accept the starting-point of the *Cogito* arrived at by the mature Descartes of the *Meditations* contemplating in his rocking chair before the fire, but rather asks the genetic question, "How did René Descartes become a thinking self?" The answer is that he developed his selfhood, or more accurately, his personhood, in relation with other persons very early in life: the reality of others—his world of other persons and things—is just as self-evident as his own existence though he probably did not recognize this because of his matured powers of abstraction and because of a lack of memory of his own psychological genesis. A metaphysics which recognizes otherness can spring the solipsistic trap and thereby deal more cogently with problems that are essentially concerned with interpersonal relations, the most pressing problems in the world today.

PERSONS, RELIGION, AND MARXISM

Because Marx emphasized community too, it is not surprising that Macmurray became very interested in Marxism once the writings of the young Marx were published in 1932. He began studying them after attending a religion conference where it was decided that to understand Christianity the conferees must first understand communism (which was then not distinguished from "Marxism"). Macmurray found communism far less opposed to Christianity than was usually thought. In fact, he became so enthusiastic about it that, although he never identified himself as a Marxist, he called for the communist approach to economics in *The Philosophy of Communism* and wrote several other articles and books on the subject, two of which argued explicitly for the possibility of a synthesis of Christianity and communism—an issue that has only become "respectable" over the last ten years or so.[2] Despite Marx's rejection of religion, Macmurray viewed the Russian experiment of the 1930's and early 1940's with great interest, but grew disillusioned when it became clear to him that, as he put it in *Self as Agent*, "in communist practice the personal is subordinated to the functional to a point at which the defence of the personal becomes itself a criminal activity."[3]

The basic appeal of Marx's thought for Macmurray was its stress on action and social relations. For both the criterion of validity is to be found in the reality encountered in action, not thought or ideas taken by themselves. But although both philosophers were strongly opposed to idealism, Macmurray refused to go to the opposite extreme of reductionistic materialism. Furthermore, he felt Marx had not amply appreciated one of the insights of his own doctrine, viz., that "the real substance of society is persons in relation."[4] That human personality is essentially social implies that true community is necessary for every person if that person is to develop properly as an individual. Marx and his followers failed to understand that individuality and community were correlatives, although they were correct in thinking that individualism, which was at the base of the invalidity of capitalism, tended to be destructive of community. This is because institutionalized ego-centeredness prevents the individual from being able to exist in free relation with others in friendship. However important economic relations might be, the most important relations in society were those of persons to persons. This insight, only latent in communism, is absolutely basic to religion and especially to Christianity. It was the fundamental insight of Jesus.

THE CRITIQUE OF DUALISM

By the time of the Gifford Lectures Macmurray's interest in the analogies between Marxism and Christianity had somewhat abated, largely because of the failure of existing communist states to provide for the personal dimension of life. In its place was another interest, present in his earlier work but now much more definitively presented. This was the synthesizing character of religion, whereby it integrates as well as complements all the other modes of human action. Or as he put it in 1961, the function of religion is "to maintain and extend, to deepen and develop human community."[5] Religion is usually conceived of too narrowly: if it is taken to be a primarily intellectual activity it is being confused with science; if it is considered essentially contemplative it is being mistaken for art. The emphasis on the theoretical in traditional Western thought has led to these confusions. The Greeks taught that the life of contemplation was the best life to be sought, and that all practical activity was merely a means to the attainment of the "good life" of contemplation. Knowledge thus became an end in itself, sought for its own sake and not for the action to which it could lead. Descartes reaffirmed this approach when he defined man as a thinking thing, a mind, choosing to leave all reference to man's body out of the definition. Indeed, body and soul for Plato are mutually exclusive, as are body and mind for Descartes. Essentially the same dichotomy can be found throughout the history of Western philosophy, according to Macmurray. This dualism keeps philosophy from coming to grips with reality because it encourages a radical disconnection between reflective activity and practical life.

Yet the withdrawal from the practical world is defined by these same philosophers as a withdrawal into reality, so the theoretical standpoint prevents them from confronting true reality, and the only way for philosophy to get back to reality and to effectiveness is by rejecting idealistic epistemology and affirming the reality and primacy of action.

The withdrawal of philosophy into the thinking self, away from direct contact with others in practical action, is a denial of human nature, for man is by nature a communal, even more than a merely social, being. Since communion or fellowship is at the center of religion, religion cannot be adequately described by any philosophy which does not take action as primary and personal relations as absolutely fundamental in human nature. Religion is concerned with the relations of persons, and with understanding the nature of reality as a whole. This latter involves withdrawal from practical activity into reflection, to be sure, but this withdrawal is made in order to improve personal relations through a better understanding of the world, which includes the self. Legitimate religious contemplation has as its goal fellowship, not expression for its own sake, as is the case in art. Religion is the ultimate human activity and is completely natural to man, requiring neither spiritual removal from reality nor a suspension of belief in nature and science. It is "practical and concrete, unlike science and art, for it unifies the intellectual and emotional sides of our nature as a way of living."[6] Science and art find completion in their integration with religion, from which they originally emanated as specializations of the two aspects of religious reflection, viz., the intellectual and the contemplative.

The objectivity attained by science and art, each in its own way, is a kind of self-transcendence, but its reference is to an object which is not taken as personal in a personal relation. But in the going outside the self which constitutes religious self-transcendence, the center of interest resides in another person, and the fullness of this is action for another, with the person who is acting totally devoted to the other. Such a perfect love would be the "fullness of rationality," for rationality is the capacity for self-transcendence.[7] In order for self-transcendence or rationality to be complete there must be a total giving over of the self; this is only possible in caring for another person.

The community attained in religion is not only a community among persons but also one between people and the natural world. Man is dependent upon nature as well as upon other people, and thus there must be a "community of all existence."[8] There is also another, non-human person who is a member of the community of existence, and that is God, the Other Person upon whom the community itself is dependent and upon whom it acknowledges itself to be dependent in religion. God is the creator of the world and the father of all men, the infinite and personal Other who is the other term of all the personal relationships in the world put together. Religion without God is meaningless.

Religion is the result of men reflecting upon their experience of mutuality and their need for fellowship and unity. It is empirical because it is founded in experience and its doctrines can be put to the test of verification in experience:

> In the scientific field, . . . one does not throw science over-board because a favourite theory has been shown to be in-valid. Why should it be different in religion? Could we not hope that through testing and modification we should arrive at a religion which science need not be ashamed to serve?[9]

Religious doctrines can be tested for validity by putting their practical meanings into practice. Any doctrines which cannot be put to the test cannot be said to be meaningful, not to mention true or false; and if anyone refuses to allow a doctrine to be put to a practical test but rather demands that it be believed without verification of any sort, he is asking for irrational belief. Dogmatism is therefore irrational. Philosophy and theology therefore have the same function, and must be equally empirical in their orientation. There is therefore no reason for their distinction. Philosophy must be theology without the biases of traditional theology—"theology which has abandoned dogmatism, and has become in a new and wider sense a Natural Theology."[10]

The Primacy of the Personal

Macmurray's empiricism is radical because its main theme, the primacy of the personal, is founded on the fundamental nature of the personal itself. There is no category which serves to render the personal intelligible; rather, the concept of the personal renders all else intelligible. If Descartes had taken the standpoint of the total experience of action instead of pure thought, a derivative of experience, in investigating the matters he subjected to his methodic doubt he would have had to admit that the person in action is just as immediately bound up with the thing acted upon or with as he is with his own consciousness, or more so. This immediate unity between the self and his world Macmurray calls immediate experience or primary knowledge. It is an un-mediated, pre-conceptual immersion of the self in the reality of action in the world. Immediate experience is continuous, gath-ered up into a whole, not fragmented as it becomes when it is reflected upon. Thought destroys the unity of immediate experience by pushing aside everything in it but what is to be concentrated on, but action *is* immediate experience. At first a child knows only immediately, and learns to reflect later. What it knows is primarily its mother (or person functioning as mother). Through this personal experience it develops a knowledge of self and non-personal things, living and non-living. Selfhood develops in personal action:

> I know myself only as I reveal myself to you; and you know yourself only in revealing yourself to me. Thus, self-revelation is at the same time self-discovery.[11]

There is a total dependence at the beginning of life, maturing into an interdependence with others. Macmurray demonstrates that a genetic analysis of consciousness is necessary for philosophy; by failing to perform one Descartes led philosophy in a direction that had to be reversed.

Macmurray knew Kant's philosophy well and was impressed with his failure to solve satisfactorily the question of the nature of the relation of man to the world. Although he did philosophize from the theoretical standpoint of the "I think" or transcendental unity of apperception, Kant nevertheless saw that to give credence to the claim that there was a real world of action he would have to declare practical rather than theoretical reason to be primary—which he did in his *Critique of Practical Reason*. But for Kant this declaration was revolution enough: virtually nothing more was made of the principle he had discovered. Macmurray decided to try to do something more with the principle of the primacy of the practical, and the result was his own new Copernican Revolution.

Unlike G. E. Moore, who said that it was the work of other philosophers and not the world or the sciences which was his "main stimulus to philosophise," Macmurray has always been motivated by problems related to the lack of community in the world. Because these problems have to do with interpersonal relations, and because traditional philosophies could not handle such a concept, he had to strike out on his own. In the process of establishing a firmer rational base for religion he not only developed a new metaphysics or philosophy of religion, but also a new metaphilosophy or philosophy of philosophy. That others have since begun to do the same sort of thing independently of Macmurray in no way diminishes the importance of his work. On the contrary, it enhances it.

Footnotes

[1] *Persons in Relation* (London, 1961), p. 206.

[2] Cf. especially *Creative Society: A Study of the Relation of Christianity to Communism* (London, 1935), and "Christianity and Communism: Towards a Synthesis," in *Christianity and the Social Revolution*, ed. J. Lewis, K. Polanyi and D. Kitchin (New York, 1936).

[3] *The Self as Agent* (London, 1957), p. 30.

[4] *The Philosophy of Communism* (London, 1933), pp. 53, 65.

[5] *Religion, Art, and Science* (Liverpool, 1961), p. 54.

[6] *Freedom in the Modern World* (London, 1932, 1936), p. 53.

[7] *Search for Reality in Religion*, p. 28.

[8] *Religion, Art, and Science*, p. 58.

[9] *Search for Reality in Religion*, p. 14.

[10] *Persons in Relation*, p. 224; cf. *Religion, Art, and Science*, p. 71, and *Search for Reality in Religion*, p. 58.

[11] *Persons in Relation*, p. 120.

The Writings of John Macmurray/

COMPILED BY ALBERT H. NEPHEW

"Is Art a Form of Apprehension or a Form of Expression?" *Proceedings of the Aristotelian Society (PAS), Supp.* 5 (1925): 173-89.

"Christianity—Pagan or Scientific," *The Hibbert Journal* 24 (1926): 421-33.

"The Function of Experiment in Knowledge," *PAS,* 27 (1926-27): 193-212.

"Government by the People," *Journal of Philosophical Studies* 2 (1927): 532-43.

"Beyond Knowledge" and "Objectivity in Religion," in *Adventure: The Faith of Science and the Science of Faith,* ed. B. Streeter. New York: Macmillan, 1928.

"Time and Change," *PAS, Supp.* 8 (1928): 143-61.

"The Principle of Personality in Experience," *PAS* 29 (1928-29): 316-30.

"The Unity of Modern Problems," *Journal of Philosophical Studies* 4 (1929): 162-79.

"Introduction," in *Immanuel Kant's Lectures on Ethics,* trans. Louis Infield. London: Methuen, 1930.

"The Conception of Society," *PAS* 31 (1930-31): 127-42.

Learning to Live. London: n.p., 1931.

Freedom in the Modern World. London: Faber, 1932; 2nd ed. rev., 1936; reprinted 1968.

"What is Philosophy?" *PAS, Supp.* 11 (1932) : 48-67.

"The Grith Fyrd Idea," in *The Grith Fyrd Idea.* Godschill: The Order of Woodcraft Chivalry, 1933.

Interpreting the Universe. London: Faber, 1933.

The Philosophy of Communism. London: Faber, 1933.

Some Makers of the Modern Spirit. London: Methuen, 1933; reprinted, 1968.

Creative Society: A Study of the Relation of Christianity to Communism. London: Faber, 1935.

"The Dualism of Mind and Matter," *Philosophy* 10 (1935) : 264-78.

"The Nature and Function of Ideologies," and "The Nature of Philosophy," and "The New Materialism," in J. M. Murry, et al., *Marxism.* London: Chapman and Hall, 1935.

"The Nature of Reason," *PAS* 35 (1934-35) : 137-48.

Reason and Emotion. London: Faber, 1935; 2nd ed. 1962.

"Christianity and Communism: Towards a Synthesis," and "The Early Development of Marx's Thought," in *Christianity and the Social Revolution,* ed. J. Lewis et al. New York: Scribner's, 1936.

The Structure of Religious Experience. London: Faber, 1936.

The Clue to History. London: Student Christian Movement Press, 1938.

"A Philosopher Looks at Psychotherapy," in *Individual Psychology Medical Pamphlets: No. 20.* London: Daniel, 1938.

"What Is Action?" *PAS, Supp.* 17 (1938) : 69-85.

The Boundaries of Science: A Study in the Philosophy of Psychology. London: Faber, 1939.

"Freedom in the Personal Nexus," in *Freedom: Its Meaning,* ed. R. Anschen. New York: Harcourt, 1940.

Challenge to the Churches: Religion and Democracy. London: Kegan Paul, 1941.

Constructive Democracy. London: Faber, 1943.

Foundation of Economic Reconstruction: A Plea for the Synthesis of the Spiritual and Material Aspects of Life. London: National Peace Council, 1943.

"Functions of a University," *Political Quarterly* 15 (1944): 277-85.

Idealism Against Religion. London: Lindsey, 1944.

Through Chaos to Community? London: National Peace Council, 1944.

A Crisis of Culture: The USSR and the West. London: National Peace Council, 1947.

Conditions of Freedom. London: Faber, 1949.

"Some Reflections on the Analysis of Language," *Philosophical Quarterly* 1 (1951): 319-37.

"Concerning the History of Philosophy," *PAS, Supp*. 25 (1951): 1-24.

"Prolegomena to a Christian Ethic," *Scottish Journal of Theology* 9 (1956): 1-13.

The Form of the Personal. Vol. 1: *The Self as Agent*. London: Faber, 1957.

"Developing Emotions," *Saturday Review* 41 (1958): 22.

The Form of the Personal. Vol. 2: *Persons in Relation*. London: Faber, 1961.

Religion, Art, and Science. Liverpool: Liverpool U. Press, 1961.

To Save From Fear. London: Friends Home Service Committee, 1964.

Search for Reality in Religion. London: George Allen and Unwin, 1965.

Notes on Contributors/

W.H.F. BARNES is Emeritus Professor of the Universities of Manchester and Liverpool, and was Gifford Lecturer at the University of Edinburgh in 1969 and 1970. From 1963-69 he served as Vice-Chancellor of Liverpool University. He is the author of *The Philosophical Predicament* as well as numerous articles in *Mind, Philosophy, Philosophical Review, Proceedings of the Aristotelian Society,* etc.

A. R. C. DUNCAN is Professor of Philosophy at Queen's University at Kingston, Ontario, where he has been Head of the Department of Philosophy since 1949. He has also taught at the Universities of London and Edinburgh. His publications include *Practical Reason and Morality, Moral Philosophy,* and a translation of De Vleeschauwer's *Evolution of Kantian Thought,* as well as articles in the *Encyclopaedia Britannica* and elsewhere.

ERROL E. HARRIS is Professor of Philosophy at Northwestern University. While a visiting professor at Yale University he gave the Terry Lectures; he has also taught at the Universities of Witwatersrand (South Africa), Edinburgh, Kansas, and Connecticut College. In 1968-69 he was president of the Metaphysical Society of America. His writings include *Salvation from Despair: Spinoza's Philosophy; Hypothesis and Perception; Annihilation and Utopia; Foundations of Metaphysics in Science; The Survival of Political Man; Nature, Mind, and Modern Science; Revelation through Reason;* and other books and articles.

H.D. LEWIS is Professor of History and Philosophy at Kings College, University of London. He was a Gifford Lecturer at the University of Edinburgh in 1966-67 and 1967-68, and has taught in the United States at Bryn Mawr, Harvard Divinity School and elsewhere. His works include *Morals and New Theology, Morals and Revelation, Contemporary British Philosophy* (ed.), *Clarity is not Enough* (ed.), *World Religions, Dreaming and Experience, The Elusive Mind, Our Experience of God, Self and Immortality,* and articles in numerous philosophical and theological journals. He is also the editor of the Muirhead Library of Philosophy.

JOHN MACMURRAY is Emeritus Professor of Edinburgh University. His best-known work is his Gifford Lectures of 1953-54, *The Self as Agent* and *Persons in Relation*. A full bibliography is appended to Albert Nephew's intellectual portrait of Macmurray above.

ALBERT H. NEPHEW is an associate professor of philosophy at the College of St. Scholastica, Duluth, Minnesota. His doctoral dissertation (Marquette University) was *Philosophy is Theology: The Nature and Function of Philosophy according to John Macmurray*. He is presently writing a book on ethics as well as an educational module for an Environmental Education Project, for which he is a values consultant. He would welcome corrections or additions to the Macmurray bibliography printed here, including secondary material.

BASIL O'LEARY is Visiting Professor at the University of Notre Dame, where he teaches economics and coordinates the Program in Non-Violence. He was chairman of the department of economics at St. Mary's College (Winona, Minnesota) until 1969, when he transferred to the Wisconsin State Correctional System, where he served a sentence as a peace felon for burning draft files as a member of the Milwaukee Fourteen. He has graduate degrees in both economics and philosophy, and has written essays on law, his prison reflections, education, love, and other topics which have appeared in *Continuum* and elsewhere.

AXEL STERN is presently Visiting Professor of Philosophy at the University of Tübingen, as well as Senior Lecturer at the University of Hull. He was educated in Europe, settled in England in 1950, and married the Belgian philosopher Suzanne Gillet in 1969. His writings include *Poème métaphysique en prose; Morale de la liberté, L'existentialisme contre l'existence, Le vrai en art et en science; Metaphysical Reverie; The Science of Freedom;* and *Creative Ethics* (forthcoming), as well as articles in *Archives de Philosophie, Proceedings of the Aristotelian Society,* etc.

THOMAS E. WREN is Associate Professor of Philosophy at Loyola University of Chicago. His writings include *Agency and Urgency: The Nature of Moral Obligation* and articles in *Ethics* and elsewhere. He is also editor of the New University Press Studies in Ethics and Society.